Just Do It!

The Story of a Boy
Who Lived up to his Name

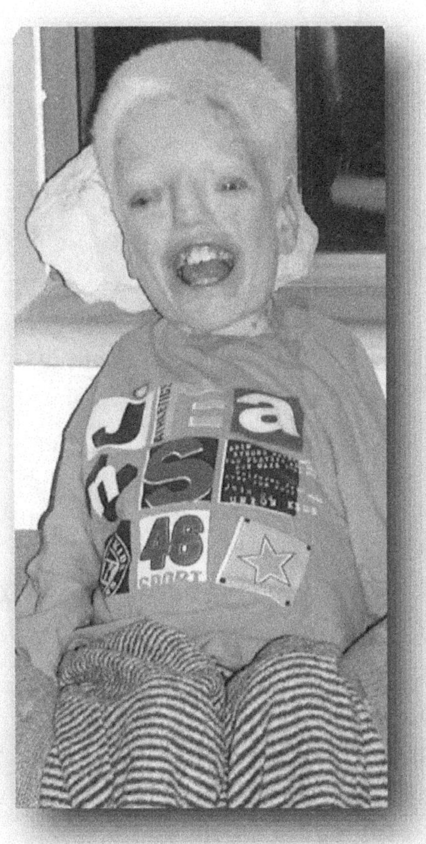

Petra van der Zande

ISBN 978 965 7542 48 4

Unless otherwise stated, Scripture quotations are taken from THE HOLY BIBLE, NEW INTERNATIONAL VERSION.

Previous publications:
First edition May 2009
Second edition June 2009
Third edition September 2009
Fourth edition August 2010
Fifth edition December 2016

Summary:
Inspirational life story of a multi handicapped Arab foster child living with a Christian family in Jerusalem, Israel.

CONTACT INFORMATION

You can order a copy of this book through www.lulu.com

Email: tsurtsinapublications@gmail.com

Website: www.tsurtsinapublications.com

Blog: http://nailtheacquirer.blogspot.com

Na'il, our foster son,
passed away suddenly on
February 4, 2009.
He was fourteen years old.

*"But something
extraordinary
happens to us
when sharing our personal hurts
also helps heal
someone else's pain."*

Kristi Holl

It is our prayer that this story,
a 'Celebration' of Na'il's life,
will be a comfort and encouragement to many.

Table of Contents

Table of Contents

What's in a Name?

Na'il means "acquirer"
It means to get or gain
by one's own efforts or actions.
Synonyms are: achieve, amass, attain,
collect, earn, gain, gather, get, obtain, pick up,
procure, realize, receive, secure, win.

His biological parents couldn't have given him
a more fitting name!

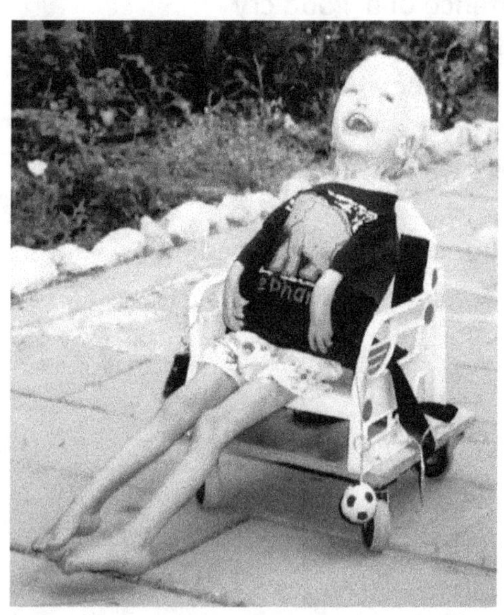

1

"I know the plans that I have for you, declares the LORD. They are plans for peace and not disaster, plans to give you a future filled with hope." Jeremiah 29:11 (God's Word translation 1995)

"Israel? What on earth can we do there?" I exclaimed while thinking, *that irksome country?* It came in reaction to a remark from my husband Wim (Bill) that he was under the impression that God wanted us to serve Him there. After having labored for more than three years as caretakers of our church in Amsterdam, I too felt that God was preparing us for something new. Israel however was out of the question.

"Lord, we'd love to serve You somewhere in the line of Open Doors, or in a Christian bookshop," I prayed. "I'll go anywhere but Israel!"

While praying for guidance and answers, which were slow in coming (or so we thought), we followed the desires of our hearts. And the Lord, in His mercy and loving-kindness, let us flounder. Whatever avenue we tried, all the doors stayed tightly shut.

Six months later, confused and discouraged, we desperately prayed,

"Where do you want us to go, Lord?"

Again, Israel came to Wim's mind. This time, we decided to listen to what God had been trying to tell us all along.

"OK, Lord," I said, "If this is really You speaking, then you must change my heart and give me a love for those people."

It was the kind of prayer God had been waiting for. Of course, He answered it.

We began to read the Bible in a new light, and learned about God's plan for His people. Isaiah 40:1 spoke to our hearts: "Comfort, comfort my people, says your God." Somehow, we knew that our task in Israel was connected to that verse.

One day I watched the Sound of Music, and when mother Superior sang to Maria, "Climb every mountain", I got goose-pimples.

At that moment, I knew in my heart that we were to receive our "lives calling" in Israel - a task God had prepared for us.

1989 - at the ICEJ

In July 1989, our Amsterdam home church sent us off with their blessing, but no financial support. Wim's faith didn't waver. "God will provide," he said. "He has done so in the past, and will do it again. He will confirm our calling."

We stepped out in faith and began working as volunteers at the International Christian Embassy Jerusalem. Their motto was Isaiah 40:1 and through their Social Assistance Department we often could comfort God's people in a literal way. Wim and I knew we were at the place God wanted us to be and loved it. Although the culture was completely different from Holland, we felt at home in the Promised Land.

During 1990 the threat of an Iraqi war intensified. Each Israeli citizen and tourist (the category we fell under) was issued a gasmask and received instructions on how to prepare sealed rooms. It was a frightening experience, not only for us, but also for our family in Holland.

"You're coming home, aren't you? Don't stay there," they pleaded.

"Sorry, but this is home. We don't want to leave when the going gets rough. We stay!" we replied.

January 1991 the Gulf War began. During many an air-raid siren we shivered in our sealed room, not knowing where the next scud missile (with or without poison gas) was going to fall. Israeli's were encouraged by our willingness to stay, amazed that we wanted to share their anxieties and troubles, and praised us for not jumping on the next plane home.

Just before the outbreak of the war, during an evening service in church I had been strangely touched by a mother putting her arm around her daughter. *Adoption* flashed through my mind. I thought that was strange, because until then, our childlessness never had been an issue. *Why now? Is it because my friend is pregnant with her first child?* I wondered.

When Wim and I began to pray about it, confirmations began to pour in, one after the other. "I wouldn't be surprised if the Lord has a child waiting for us in the wings," Wim said.

But what kind of child? I wondered. *Is it to be a baby, older child, mentally or physically handicapped, or both?* We only knew we had to look for a child nobody wanted; a precious human being to whom we could be an 'Ambassador of Love'.

I wrote a letter to Alyn Hospital, and to our amazement, two days later a social worker called us.

"We may have a child for you," the Social Worker said.

Some parents are not able to accept the fact their baby is handicapped. During the 1980's, it often happened that they abandoned their special needs child. Unlike biological parents, we choose for a handicapped child. With joy, anticipation, full of hope and faith we jumped straight into the deep. Of course, there was also trepidation.

Our Hebrew vocabulary was very basic. *How are we going to communicate with a Hebrew speaking four-year-old?* I wondered.

It took almost a year before Moshiko was ready to come and live with us. The physically disabled and emotionally troubled boy turned our lives upside down. Moshiko had been abandoned at birth, and on the card announcing his 'homecoming' in December 1991 we wrote the text: *"Though my father and mother forsake me, the Lord will receive me."* Psalm 27:10.

Fahima (a four-year-old Bedouin girl) joined our family exactly one year later, in December 1992. Her homecoming card read: *"God sets the lonely in families."* Psalm 68:6

In 1994 Nadia (Fahima's cousin) re-entered our lives with a bang. Aged seven, she was a big challenge to the extended household.

(In 1990 we had formed a community with another Dutch couple, who by now had two sons.) Multi-handicapped and deaf Nadia could only shout and yell, and acted like a wild horse.

We learned the basics of Hebrew sign language, and when she enrolled in the school for the deaf, Nadia gradually began to settle down. For this special girl, we received a promise from 1 Corinthians 1:27, *"But God chose what is foolish in the world to shame the wise; God chose what is weak in the world to shame the strong."*

Without realizing it, God began using our special family to comfort those around us. People not only were amazed by the progress the children made, but also wondered how we managed.

"Are you Christians?" Israelis sometimes bluntly asked. "You must be," they reasoned. "We wouldn't be willing to do the work you do!"

Others called us 'angels', which always embarrassed me. "We are not," I'd respond. "God gave us the idea, He gives the strength. We can only do it by His grace."

In May 1994, the same month Nadia joined our family, in Jerusalem another special child was born ~ Na'il. But it was only two years later that God put the desire in our hearts to open our home to another child, preferably a boy.

As always - God's timing was perfect!

2

"One thing the future can guarantee – anything can happen!"

The following story is a reconstruction of how it may have happened. I've blended Arab and Muslim customs with the facts we acquired and used fictitious names for the biological family.

Arab and Bedouin prefer to keep their possessions within the family, therefore it was normal that eighteen-year-old Mahmud married his thirteen-year-old cousin, Sameera. On her wedding day, Sameera left her father's house in Hebron and moved in with Mahmud's parents, who lived in a small village not far from Jerusalem.

Fareed was born a year later. Mahmud's family praised Sameera for giving her husband a son and it was the mother-in-law who taught the child-mother how to take care of the infant. About a year later Sameera conceived again. She had an uneventful pregnancy and when the contractions started, Mahmud drove his wife to a hospital in Jerusalem.

Having a baby was women's work and Islam forbids men to attend a birth - they wouldn't have wanted to be there anyhow. The moment the baby was born, a hush fell over the delivery room. Immediately the nurse covered the baby and whisked it away.

Unable to understand Hebrew, the frantic young mother didn't know what happened. Nobody explained anything to her, and she wondered if perhaps the baby had died. But she had heard a pitiful cry. The sixteen-year-old mother was horrified when an Arabic speaking nurse told her she had given birth to a deformed baby.

Na'il (acquirer, earner) as they named him, had a combination of two rare syndromes, resulting in strange facial features, no shoulders and due to a lack of muscles, a very thin body. A few weeks later the hospital told the distressed parents to take Na'il home. Sameera dreaded having to pick up 'Allah's curse'.

The neighborhood women were curious to see the baby everyone whispered about. Those who dared to look quickly turned away in fright, shock or revulsion. Fareed however, liked his little brother, who cried most of the time.

Ashamed by the people's stares and whispers, Sameera cringed each time she had to bring Na'il for a medical check-up. Not wanting to face the constant humiliation, she began to cover Na'il's face with a cloth diaper when she took him outside. Feeling revulsion to hold her son, the baby spent his days on a mattress in a dark room, his little spindly legs pulled up in fetal position.

Two years passed in which Na'il didn't grow much – the cheap, regular baby formula didn't give him enough nourishment. He never learned to sit or walk - he just lay on the floor, always in the same position, causing his legs to contracture. Shut up in his dark and quiet (he was also deaf) world, the only way Na'il could express his unhappiness was by excessive crying. It drove Sameera nuts. Spanking only made it worse.

Then came the day his parents took him for a belated check-up to Alyn hospital in Jerusalem. The shocked doctor looked at the non-stop crying, underdeveloped, undernourished and neglected child. Na'il screamed when she touched the obviously swollen lower leg.

"What happened?" she asked the father.

Mahmud looked at his wife, who shrugged.

"His leg is broken," the doctor said. "Na'il needs to stay here. We'll start intensive treatment."

During their six-months stay in the Alyn hospital, Sameera befriended an older Arabic mother who obviously loved and accepted her disabled daughter. Na'il not only underwent several operations but also joined a toddlers group in the hospital. Gradually, his life began to change for the better.

Pregnant again, Sameera was unable to cope with the problems she had to face alone. She told the social worker to place Na'il in an institution - she didn't want him any longer.

But God had a plan for Na'il's life! First, there had been the doctor. She had saved Na'il from certain death by admitting him to Alyn.
And there was Koos, the Dutch physiotherapist, who worked with him after the operations. From the first time that he interacted with the child, Koos knew that Na'il was a special child with lots of potential.

The third person who played an important role was the social worker, who didn't believe that he belonged in Saint Vincent, the place 'hopeless' cases ended up. She was determined to find a foster family for him. "Where do I find a family willing to take a child like Na'il?" she asked a colleague.

"Try Wim and Petra," the woman suggested. "They may know other Christian couples who are willing to become foster parents."

3

"For a time, will come when your innermost voice will speak to you, saying: "This is my path; here I shall find peace. I will pursue this path, come what may."" W.E. Sangster

Fostering three special needs children was never easy. Small and big sacrifices were part of the 24/7 job. Still, it was a fulfilling, God-given ministry with its good and bad days. Two thriving Bedouin girls and a Jewish boy - what more could we want? Another boy, perhaps?

Already for some time Wim and I had been thinking about a fourth child, but each time we thought a door opened, it shut in our faces.

"Lord," we prayed, "you know our hearts. Please, send us the right child."

During the first months of 1997 the desire for another child grew more intense. Perhaps this time we should consider adoption, I thought.

Thursday, June 26. "Today I'm going to call the social worker and tell her we want another child," I told Wim that morning.

However, before I had a chance to contact the woman, a phone-call changed the course of our lives. "Do you happen to know a family who would be willing to foster a disabled, three-year-old, Arab boy?" a social worker from Alyn asked.

"Yes! We would love to!" I exclaimed.

The flabbergasted woman provided more details.

"I'll call you back soon." I promised.

Wim wasn't surprised, for the day before he had been strangely touched when he saw someone wearing a T-Shirt which said "Just-do-it". "Just do it, Petra!" was all he said.

A few hours later, the social worker briefed us about the little boy.

"Tests show that his present developmental stage is like a four-month-old child," she began. "But everybody believes he has enormous potential."

There was no need to convince us, we would have taken him anyhow. Excited, Wim and I followed the social worker to the *Maon* (Day-care center for toddlers). Colorful cots lined the wall of the spacious room where I noticed a young Arab woman sitting on a mattress. A few small children were either sitting in special chairs or playing on the vinyl floor. One of them was a tiny, white-haired boy, who passively lay on his side, staring into space. Before entering the class, the social worker had warned us. "The first time you see Na'il, you'll be shocked."

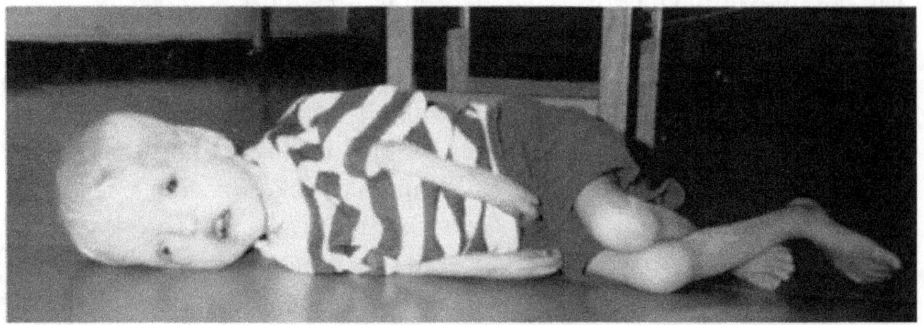

June 26,1997 - the first time we met Na'il

She was right. We experienced a short-lived jolt, but then, as we looked past the empty blue eyes, the strange facial features, and the extremely thin arms with tiny, claw-like hands, we saw a helpless child, in need of tender loving care. Compassion filled our hearts and eyes to overflowing.

The visit was short. In broken Hebrew, the Arab woman who happened to be his mother Sameera, said hello, shook our hands, and took Na'il home with her. We collected our other children from their classes in Alyn and tried to prepare them for a new brother.

Impatiently, we waited for Sunday's follow-up meeting with Widad, the social worker assigned to Na'il. "I'll set things in motion," she promised.

"Can you please inform the ministry of Social Welfare," I asked. "They need to approve the fact we're planning to take in another child."

"Don't worry. I'll take care of that too."

A hectic week followed, filled with end-of-the-school-year parties and the beginning of the summer-school schedule. When the holidays began, Fahima and I went every morning to spend some time with Na'il in the *Maon*. I was wonderful to see the dedication of the staff as they worked with these very young, handicapped children.

Four days later, Widad approached me. "Sameera asks if you are able to take Na'il for the weekend. They plan to visit relatives and don't want to take Na'il along."
What a question! Of course, we wanted to take him!

A 'wet' welcome from the dogs

Because Na'il was deaf and unable to understand sign language, we couldn't explain nor prepare him for his outing. The fact that strangers took him didn't seem to bother him.

Our new family member received a wet welcome - the dogs danced, whined and licked his face. The little boy smiled!

He woke up cranky from a nap.
"Perhaps he's hungry?" Na'il refused the bottle.
"I'll take him for a walk with the dogs."

Wim returned home with a changed child. It was obvious that everything was new and exciting for him – the trees, the clouds, even the wind in his face. No wonder, for those basic pleasures had always been denied.

Scooting on his back, the little boy happily explored the house, emptying paper baskets and investigating everything within his reach. The other children interacted nicely with him and he seemed to enjoy their attention.

It was time for bed. Whatever we tried, he kept crying and refused to go to sleep. We became desperate.

"Perhaps a car-ride will do the trick," Wim suggested around midnight.

At first, the night-sights were exciting too, but after driving around for half an hour, Na'il finally fell asleep. And thankfully didn't wake up when we put him into bed.

Shabbat (Saturday) came and it felt as if the little boy always had been with us - he fit perfectly into our family.

"This time, no night-light!" I told Wim that evening. Na'il cried for about ten minutes, fell asleep and only awoke at 6 a.m.

Sunday is a normal work-day in Israel. Knowing he would return to his biological family I dreaded taking him back to the *Maon*. The house felt empty without the curious little boy.

Shopping for baby-sized, suitable clothes proved quite a challenge. And what kind of toys could one buy for a disabled child who, instead of his hands, used his feet? Our other children were much older when they joined our family, and I didn't have a clue what Na'il liked.

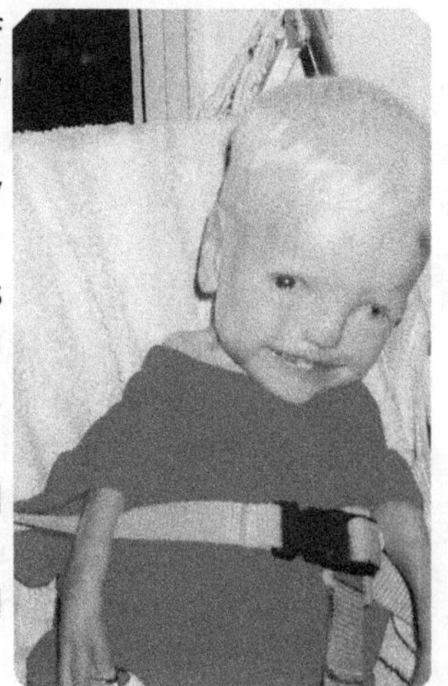

Proudly I showed the pictures we'd taken of Na'il's first visit. We noticed that everybody who knew Na'il, loved him.

"He's such a special boy!" we constantly heard in Alyn.

When they heard, we hoped to foster Na'il as well, everyone reacted positive and enthusiastic.

The social worker passed on Sameera's second request to take Na'il for the weekend.

"Are you sure?" Widad probably wondered how we survived the first visit.

"Of course! We are thrilled!"

Because the Arab population has their day off on Friday, we took Na'il home on Thursday afternoon. Na'il chortled when Fahima acted funny. He showed his excitement by 'fluttering' with his arms, especially when he realized it was time for a bath. This became his life-long most favorite activity. We noticed Na'il played with everything - from kitchen utensils to cardboard boxes - except toys. The garden swing, the walks in the buggy, sitting in the rocker - he loved it all. From behind the screen door he still could watch the sky and the trees.

Though he avoided eye contact, he often blessed us with a shy smile. Without the night-light, Na'il fell asleep after a short crying spell. We were very grateful that Jerusalem-by-night was something of the past.

On Sunday morning, it was with pain in my heart that I returned Na'il to Alyn. In the afternoon, I returned to pick up our other children, and saw Na'il in his car seat, waiting to be transported home with the other Maon children. Being unable to speak, he quietly watched us with a terrible sadness in his eyes. He understands he's not coming with us! My heart wept for him.

Compared to our other foster children, the whole process with Na'il went much faster. Still, we had to be patient, and Na'il had to endure heartbreak when he couldn't go home with us.

But God was gracious to the little boy, and he didn't have to suffer too long.

Plans had been made for a holiday in Netanya the end of July. My bold request to take Na'il along was granted and we had a wonderful week! The pool near the high-rise building became a favorite activity. When he wasn't in the water, or lying in the grass, Na'il loved to sit in his buggy and just watch everything around him.

To protect his very sensitive skin against the burning son, we parked his buggy under a giant umbrella. He loved to watch it flap in the wind. His love for umbrellas probably originates from that first Netanya holiday.

My heart made a little jump when I saw him smile, or heard a burst of laughter when Wim tickled his belly.

For most of his life Na'il had been in a horizontal position, and the doctor wanted him to learn to sit, which was very unpleasant for him. Three times a day, while sitting next to him on the floor, Wim tried to distract him with games and activities. Those 20 minutes seemed very long indeed!

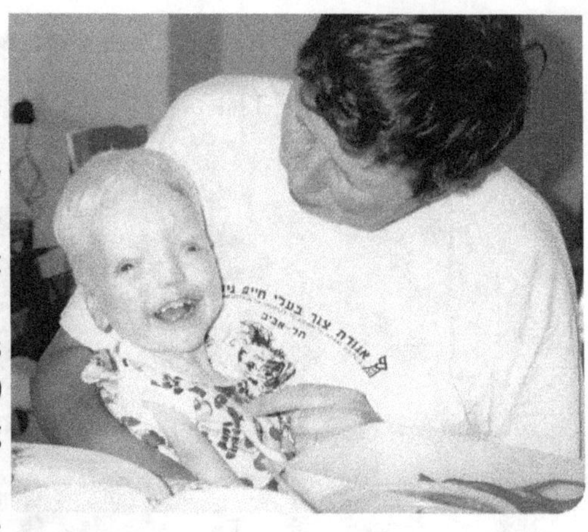

The week in Netanya ended.
Will he have to go back to his biological parents again? I wondered. We already loved the little boy; felt he belonged to our family. How will he handle the emotional turmoil if he is to be sent back and forth?

But... I needn't to have worried, for the 24th of July turned out to be the day Na'il had come home to stay!
Like we had done with the other children, for Na'il we also chose an appropriate Bible verse. It was like a prayer for his new life with us,
"I will repay you for the years the locusts have eaten..." (Joel 2:25)

In August, we travelled north to spend ten days at kibbutz Kfar haNassi. The kibbutz children were curious (in a positive way) about the funny looking child. Na'il felt they accepted him and to our relief and amazement he opened to them.

Because even a children's wheelchair was too big for Na'il, we had found another way to get him off the floor ~ a booster seat attached to a piece of wood with big wheels. It was the perfect (and cheapest) solution, enabling him to freely (and we thought safely) move around to explore his surroundings. One morning I found him stuck in the bushes when his 'scooter', as we called it, had skidded from the concrete path and he ended up on his side. Unable to move he patiently waited for someone to rescue him from his precarious position.

In the morning hours, sprinklers watered the grassy fields lining the rows of kibbutz houses.

We knew Na'il was crazy about water, but couldn't believe our eyes when he wheeled himself onto the grass, and positioned himself in the line of the water. He had the time of his life!

We took our meals in the kibbutz's dining room and this turned out to be the only place Na'il didn't like. He wanted to be outside, not cooped up again! We tried to keep him occupied by building plastic blocks towers, which he then toppled with his head. The kibbutz members joined our laughter about the child who delighted in even the smallest things.

We returned to Jerusalem with many precious memories of that first kibbutz holiday with Na'il!

Our house lacked a spare bedroom, and for Na'il to have his own sleeping quarter we did some major re-adjustments. Up until then he slept in a camping-bed next to our bed, and the moment he saw us stir at 6 a.m. he too wanted to be up and around. Preferring he went to bed early, and not keep us awake till 11 p.m. or later, we gradually 'weaned' him off the afternoon nap.

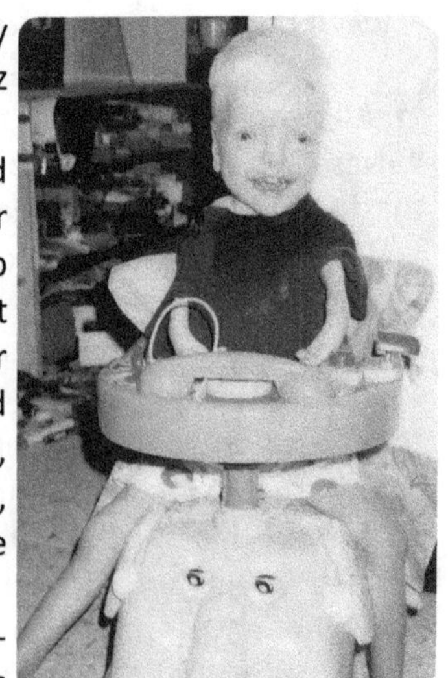

I began to see the need for a bigger car - with four children in car seats, there was no room for a second adult. The Lord knew our needs and we trusted Him to provide in due time.

4

"I thank You, Lord, that we may live in the house you prepared for us; I know Lord, that whatever happens, You'll guide us again and again..." Translation from a Dutch song

September 1. At the start of the Israeli school year Na'il was old enough to join Shula's *gan* - kindergarten. This very special woman, who also taught our other three children, seemed to always get the 'very difficult' ones.

Sameera didn't seem to miss her son at all. Na'il had come to live with us by a verbal agreement between Alyn, ourselves and the biological parents. We believed Widad had taken care of the bureaucratic side of things. We found she had not.

The ministry of Social welfare was furious that we had taken in another child. It was unheard of that a foster family cared for four very special needs children. They arranged a special meeting for September 8.

Thankfully, because Na'il had been with us for some time now, and was so well-adjusted, they decided not to remove him from our home. The administrative wheels were set in motion to make the fostering arrangement official.

Slowly, Na'il began to feel at home in Shula's *gan,* and the staff expressed their joy and amazement at the change in the previously unhappy boy. He laughed more, made 'baby' (gurgling) noises and moved around – in short: he was catching up on lost time!

One day I met a religious doctor, who had known Na'il since he was a baby. "You know, every time I see him," the doctor said, "I ask God to bless you. You've made such a difference in his life. I just can't get over the change!"

As we got to know him better, we noticed Na'il was a perceptive child. We couldn't fool him by putting something else than formula in his drinking bottle – he refused to drink it.

The bright little guy quietly observed a situation, then acted thoughtfully and in the end succeeded doing what he had in mind. Umbrellas became his most favorite and exciting toy, and for the rest he played with everything, except toys.

During the week-long holiday of Succot (the Feast of Tabernacles) school was closed. For Wim, the international Congress was always the busiest time of the year. The children loved to roam around the big congress hall and the booth area, and expecting presents from people who took pity on them. Because I helped in the Social Assistance booth, Na'il was 'cooped' up for most of the time. But the moment he saw his chance, he took off (on his back).

November 10 was a memorable day - our Social worker delivered the happy news that Na'il now officially was our foster son! Finally, we were to receive the much-needed allowance for him. God took care of us, and little Na'il was such a joy and blessing!

We didn't feel the need to move but always said that if the Lord had something better in mind, and it was presented to us, we wouldn't say no.
    In November, we moved into our new house, a 6-room cottage that was offered to us by the ICEJ's German branch. The Ramat Denia neighborhood, on the other side of the valley from where we lived, was still close to the schools, banks, health funds and the bus Wim had to take to go to work.

Na'il loved to wheel around the spacious ground floor leading to a walled-in terrace, where the dogs were kept. While the dogs were eating I always kept an eye on Na'il, but one day he came too close for the male dog's comfort. The little boy thought that being bitten in the cheek was funny and laughed about it! Not wanting to risk an infection, I took him to Hadassah hospital's Emergency room. Na'il loved the medical equipment, the doctors and nurses, even the tetanus shot!

One of the fostering rules was that the child had to visit his biological parents on a regular basis. This meant that each month Na'il had to spend a weekend with them.

Near the main post office on Jaffa road, central to both families, we said goodbye to a little boy whom we couldn't prepare for what was about to happen. As both cars were waiting side by side at the traffic light, I saw Na'il sitting on his mother's lap. My heart broke when I saw the look of utter hopelessness in his eyes. He probably thinks he returns to them for good.

I had a terrible weekend, afraid what might happen to him, feeling bereft of our little helpless boy whom I so desperately wanted to protect. We prayed for God's angels to keep an eye on him and bring him safely back to us. Na'il was so happy when he returned home. And so were we!

However, a few days after visiting his family he came down with a bug. This became a pattern. Emotionally and physically, Na'il (and we) paid a high price for each visit to his biological family.

The year 1998 began with heavy snowfall. Impassable roads made driving hazardous and people were advised to stay home so emergency services could do their job. The children loved the winter wonderland. Schools were closed, and they begged us to take them outside to play in the snow. However, after a cold and difficult walk, they agreed it was more fun to watch from the inside. Wim built four snowmen, and Na'il was upset when I took him inside, out of the cold.

A few days later, when the snow began to melt, he maneuvered his scooter under the dripping roof till he was soaking wet. The warm bath afterwards was such bliss!

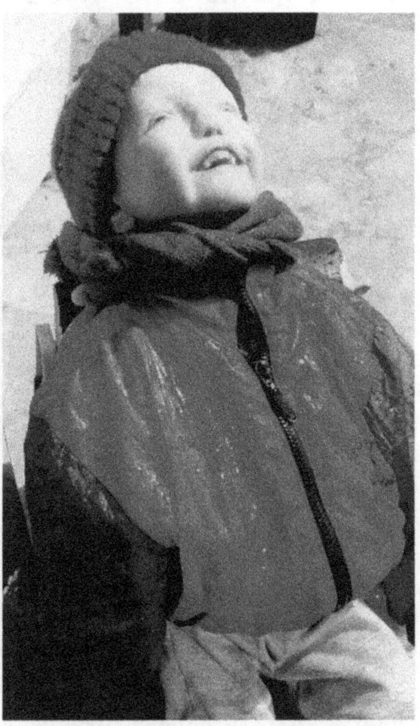

We already made plans to take the whole family to Holland in April, and now we had to get travel documents for Na'il as well. In March, we accompanied Na'il's mother to the Ministry of Interior. One of the clerks had mercy on the cranky child who wanted action, and whizzed us past the long waiting lines. With grateful hearts, we held the laissez-passé (travel document).

Our other children were Israeli citizens, so we never needed a visa for Holland. A few weeks before the trip, our travel agent reminded us that we needed a visa for Na'il, who according to his travel document, was a Jordanian citizen. (He was born on Israel's so-called West Bank.) Together with the little guy we embarked on a trip to Tel Aviv, applied for a visa at the Dutch Embassy and heard this would take at least two weeks. (Security check – and yes, even a handicapped child could be a terrorist!) Thanks to the intervention of the Dutch Ambassador we got our visa in record time.

The flight to Holland on March 31st was like a military operation. Anxiously I wondered how Na'il was going to behave during the flight, but the moment we were airborne, he fell asleep in the car seat and slept right through the 4½ hour trip. Airport personnel helped us disembark and handed us over into the open arms of waiting family members.

For three weeks, we stayed in our 'old' apartment above the church.

All the excitement and sudden changes were a bit much too for Na'il. When he began to eat less I became worried. The adjusted program suited us fine.

Patiently waiting for Wim to set the domino blocks and then he was allowed to tip over the first one - he could not get enough of the game.

Ariving at Schiphol Airport with over 120 kilos of luggage, I was relieved when the security lady remembered us from two years previous. While waiting for the delayed plane to arrive, our children played with other Israeli children while Na'il raced around in his scooter. Afraid to lose him, we constantly ran after our inquisitive little boy. Finally, it was time to board the plane.

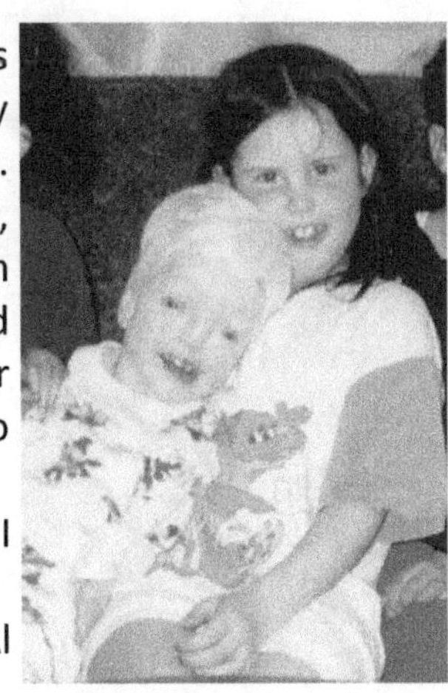
Making Dutch friends

"Business class? No, that's a mistake," I said.

"You've been upgraded by the head of El Al security," the stewardess told me. Again, we were blessed because of the children! We settled into the spacious seats, and like the first time, Na'il fell asleep the moment we were airborne.

Safely back in Jerusalem, the children instantly fell asleep in their own beds, except for Na'il. He figured he had slept enough on the plane, was excited to be back home and was ready for action. Never mind it was in the middle of the night!

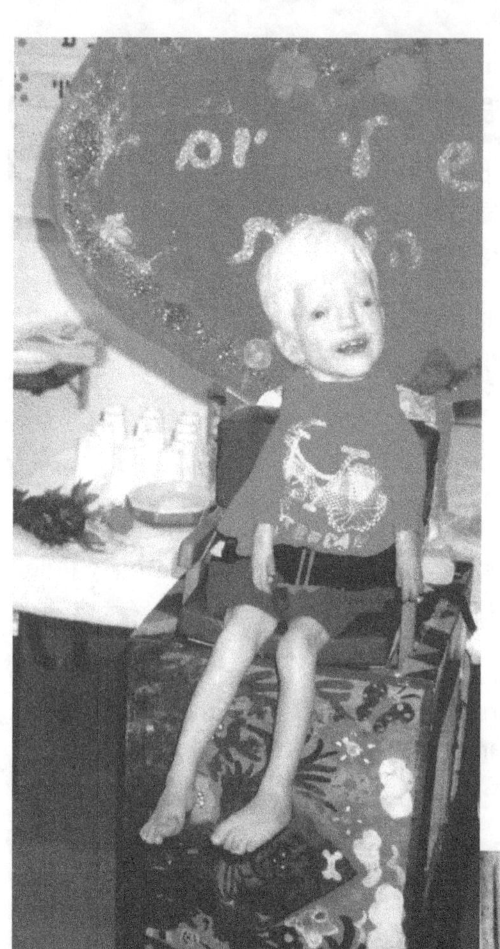

Mazal Tov leNa'il!

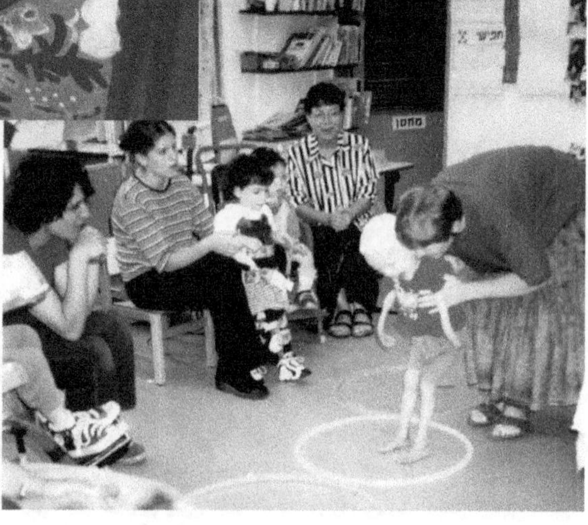

5

Overcoming new Challenges

We had left Israel in winter and returned to a heat wave.

Because it was almost Independence Day, Na'il went to school wearing a white shirt and blue trousers. Throughout Israel, similarly dressed schoolchildren attended special gatherings which begin when sirens mark minutes of silence. This year's *Yom haAtsma'ut* (Independence Day) was extra special because it was Israel's 50th birthday! Half a century of miracles too.

More celebrations followed. Na'il's 4th birthday was on May 27, but due to all the school activities around Shavuot (Pentecost) this was only celebrated in June. Na'il didn't have a clue what a birthday was, for Arabs usually don't celebrate them. His biological parents seemed to have forgotten he was born that day, for when they picked him up for a long weekend, they didn't mention it.

For me, that long Shavuot weekend was tainted with worry about Na'il's well-being. We so much hoped this would be his last long weekend. The social worker promised to find a solution that was best for the child, and not according to what the law said.

Home again, Na'il spent the first half hour racing around the house, beaming and laughing. We'd never seen him so happy and were so grateful our precious boy was back, safe and sound. How we'd missed him!

At school, Na'il's birthday was celebrated with games, balloons, candles and dancing. Lifting him in our arms was the highlight – one, two, three, four… and an extra one for the new year! Na'il didn't want us to stop! How wonderful it was to give these special children some added happiness in their lives.

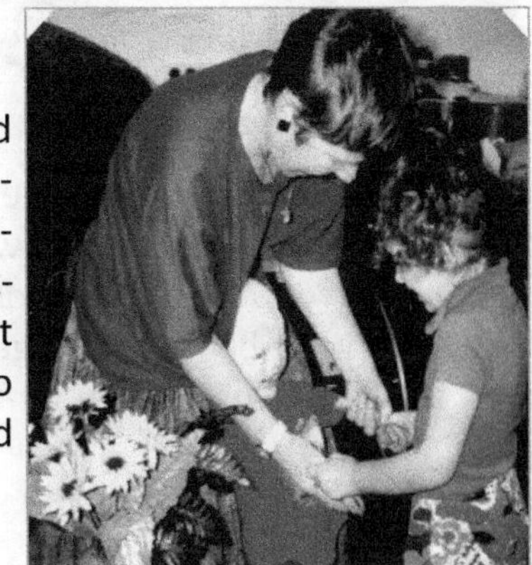

Na'il's behavior in school improved and changed for the better. Daily, the teacher's aide worked with him on the computer. He refused to make floor puzzles (with his feet), but when asked to make a jigsaw puzzle on the computer, he did it without making a mistake. They were flabbergasted!

Na'il wasn't too enthusiastic about the fitting of new hearing-aids; the hearing test wasn't a success either. What he did like was the school outing to a kibbutz. I joined them as a volunteer, for they needed one-on-one help plus extras. It was a blessing the weather wasn't too hot, for being both white-skinned, Na'il and I couldn't handle too much sun.

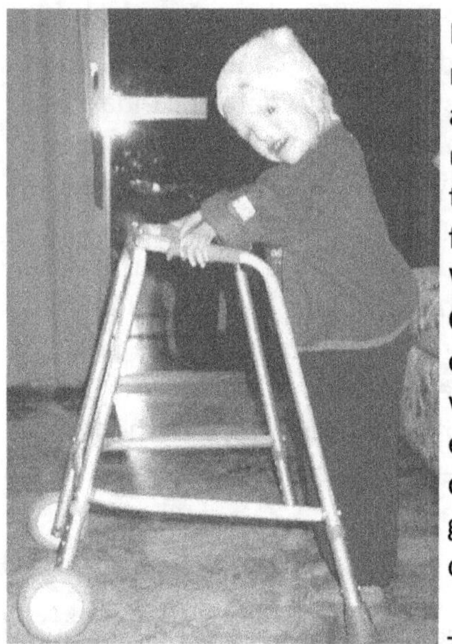

In Alyn they not only worked on his mental development, but his physical advancement as well. Na'il learned to use a walker and succeeded to walk three meters! For him, it must have felt like a marathon – such an effort! We bought him a walker for home. One afternoon Na'il first brought Wim, dozing on the couch, his shoes and with his feet dragged the walker closer. Smiling from ear to ear, he then sat down on the couch, hoping for Wim to get the hint. Who could refuse such a child?

The end of June the health-fund finally approved Na'il's long overdue dental treatment. Under full anesthesia, both front teeth were fitted with crowns and the rest was either filled or pulled. After the 'operation' we stayed on the day-care ward, and saw everyone being discharged, except for Na'il. He had swallowed a lot of blood, which made him nauseous, and refused to drink his formula.

"I can only discharge you when he starts to drink water," the doctor told me.

"But he never drinks water, only formula," I protested. Because I desperately wanted to go home, I tried to force-feed Na'il. He then began to vomit old blood.

"I'm sorry, but you'll have to stay overnight," the nurse told me.

That was a scenario I had not considered. Resigned, I followed the nurse to the children's ward where I spent a miserable night on a mattress next to Na'il, who slept like a log! Thankfully, the next morning he thirstily drank from his formula, didn't vomit and we were finally released to go home! Na'il showed his new front teeth to everyone!

Because we applied to the National Insurance Institute for a bigger car, we had to appear before a medical committee – in Tel Aviv!

The narrow corridor was filled with people waiting for the same reason. Na'il raced around in his scooter, tried all kinds of doors, entered offices - I had a hard time keeping track of him. His disappointment that I didn't let him do what he wanted was soon forgotten when his eyes fell on a man holding a walker. Na'il was determined to have that walker. Clearly embarrassed, the poor man tried to hold on to it for dear life. When Na'il didn't succeed, he found another 'victim' – a man holding a pair of crutches. Na'il tried to confiscate those as well!

I was relieved when our name was called. The committee promised to consider our request. Grateful to leave humid Tel Aviv behind we drove back to the much cooler Jerusalem. I'm sure the people in that corridor were more than happy to see us leave too.

School continued with a six-week summer program, after which we still had to figure a way how to spend the remaining two weeks' holiday.

It was wonderful to be back in Kfar Hanassi. The small kibbutz house had a living room with double bed, a bedroom for the children, a kitchenette and bathroom - a perfect place for our family, including the dogs.

The weather was very hot, so we spent our days in and around the pool. After lunch, we all had a siesta, with the result that Na'il only fell asleep after 11 p.m.

The daughter-in-law of an elderly couple had a therapeutic horse riding school on the Golan Heights. We were invited to have some fun. The children loved it, and dear Ann, after having worked in the heat the whole day, took them for a special ride. Wim and Na'il sat on horseback together and the little boy just loved it!

September came, the new school year began and Na'il was happy to be back into the daily rhythm of Shula's class.

Our new car arrived, which we named "Gideon II". In Holland we had a minibus with the name "Gideon", which had served us on several trips behind the Iron Curtain. We prayed the new Gideon would bless our special needs family. The Hyundai 100 not only had space for the buggy and wheelchairs, but the whole family as well – such luxury!

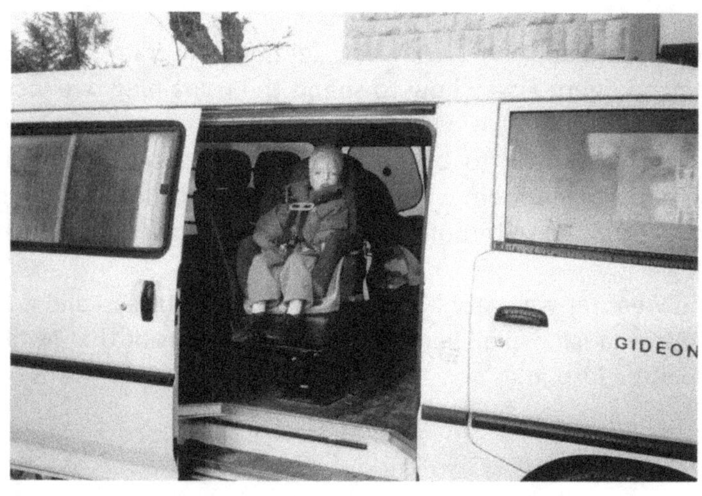

6

Becoming a Dutch TV Star

In January 1999, almost every one of the family came down with the flu. Na'il often suffered from 'one-day-bugs', causing him to vomit for one day. Most of the time, he recuperated quickly. However, when the vomiting took longer than a day, I began to worry, for he didn't have any reserves and his small, thin body was quickly dehydrated. We were grateful that Na'il recovered quickly from this flu episode.

He was our sunshine and kept amazing not only us, but also the people who worked with him.

One day, a group of Health Fund doctors came to visit Alyn and noticed Na'il. "I thought these children no longer existed," said one doctor.

Well, he did, and what a blessing he was! At school they taught him to use a motorized wheelchair with his foot, on a tricycle he cycled through the long corridors, and played table football.

At home, he 'crawled' via his back up the stairs and got into all kind of mischief in the bedrooms. He lived and was happy and thrived! We had our hands full with our little inquisitive boy, but seeing him blossom made it all so worthwhile!

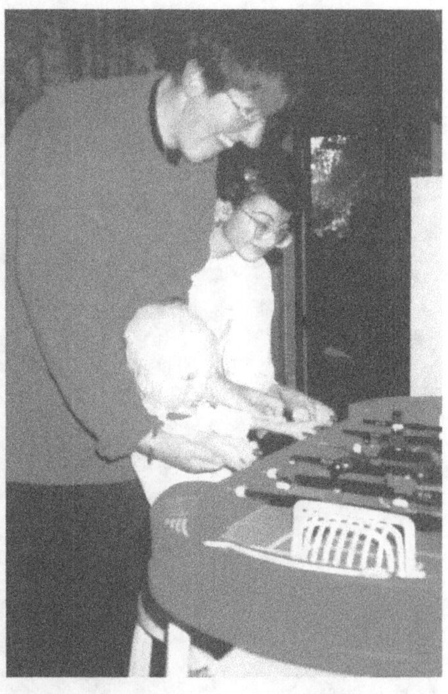

There are many ways
to 'climb' the stairs

We never forgot Na'il's 5th birthday.
A Dutch film crew wanted to interview some Dutch people living in Israel.

"We don't have time," our friends said. "Can you do it?"
At first, we weren't too happy, because the man doing the interviews was notorious for making people feel uncomfortable by his rude questions and behavior. Only because a well-known Dutch Christian would also be present, did we consent. The children had to come along, for we didn't have the luxury of baby sitters for our special needs children. Everything went so fast we had hardly time to be nervous.
That Thursday was a busy and hot day and the children were moody and cranky. Careful not to trip over the many cables that seemed to be everywhere we found the hotel room where the make-up artists went to work. I almost didn't recognize myself when she was finished. Up on the roof a film crew member explained where we had to sit and when we were supposed to come up.

"During the filming, your son must stay in his buggy for about one hour," the man said. "You think he'll manage?"
I really hoped so! We were introduced to Henk Binnendijk and Paul de Leeuw, the 'infamous' man, who soon was joking with the children.

It was time for the program to start. Waiting on the roof was an audience of about eighty Dutch people. Paul began to interview several people while the evening sun basked the Old City walls in a glowing light. And then it was our turn to take a seat between Henk and Paul. Not knowing what kind of questions Paul was going to ask us, at first, we were apprehensive. Of course, the children were the main subject and Paul showed his amazement at our trust and faith in God.

"We wanted to take in these special children that nobody wanted, because they are so close to God's Father heart," I said.
The remark received a warm applause from the audience.
When Paul heard that it was Na'il's 5th birthday, he spontaneously began to sing "Happy birthday to you", with the audience following suit.

"Oh, that's nice!" I laughed. "But Na'il is deaf, you know?"

"Ah, thus we sang for nothing!" Paul said. "Should have used our hands then…." He waved both hands.

Before we knew it, the program leader signed to Paul, "Two minutes… one minute… wrap up!"

Our ten minutes were history. We were so relieved that Paul had not made fun of us, and that the children had behaved wonderfully, even Na'il! The edited version was to be sent to Holland by satellite and aired the same evening. Later, we received many reactions from Christian friends who had watched the program. According to them, Paul had been a totally different man than his usual rude self. We were so grateful for that miracle!

During the summer holiday, we spent another ten days at Kibbutz Kfar haNassi. In front of the house was a grassy area, where Na'il loved to sit or lie in the shade. Baruch, our male dog, made friends with a fat Golden retriever. When this lovely animal came too close to Na'il for our female dog, Simmie's, liking, the usually fearful dog felt the need

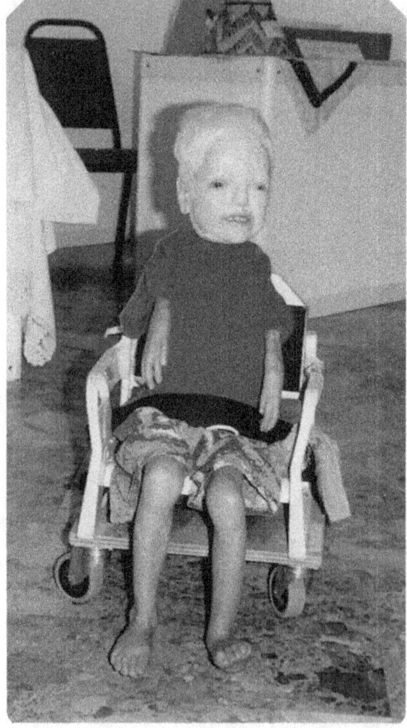

to guard Na'il like a puppy. When the silly retriever almost sat on top of Na'il (who thought that was very funny) Simmie was ready to attack him. During another visit to the therapeutic horse riding school Na'il would have loved to join the horse in the stable and even tried to stick his foot in a horse's mouth. His lack of fear amazed us, and he was happy to sit on horseback again. The smile didn't leave his face when Anne drove him and Wim around the premises.

Succot was extra busy that year, because special education didn't have their usual holiday program.

I now had to take four children with me to the Congress Hall where the oldest three participated in the youth program. Older now, Na'il refused to be confined to the small area behind the booth. I tried the crèche, but after exploring the room (and upsetting the children because of his facial features) he was ready to hit the road (corridors) again. Na'il especially liked the big elevators which were outfitted with many lights. Afraid to lose him in that vast building, we taped a sign on the back of his scooter that read, "My name is Na'il, I'm five years old and deaf! I belong to the Social Assistance Booth." It drew many smiles from pilgrims and booth holders alike. When it was time to go home I was exhausted.

Nadia needed an emergency eye operation, and as usual, I stayed with her during the hospitalization. In the evening, Wim took Na'il for a visit to the hospital. The little guy roamed the corridors or to just sat on Nadia's bed. This was the beginning of many visits to come. Na'il loved it, and became known (famous rather) to many doctors and nurses from the different wards Nadia frequented.

After having tried unsuccessfully for many years, the Interior Ministry finally granted us temporary residence. Because we now were the proud owners of an Israeli Identity card, we could become members of an Israeli Health fund, and receive other services that up until then had been out of our reach. For us, it surely had been a Chanukah miracle – *Nes Gadol Haya Poh*! (* Outside Israel, you say *"sham"* - there. In Israel, we say, *"poh"* - here.)

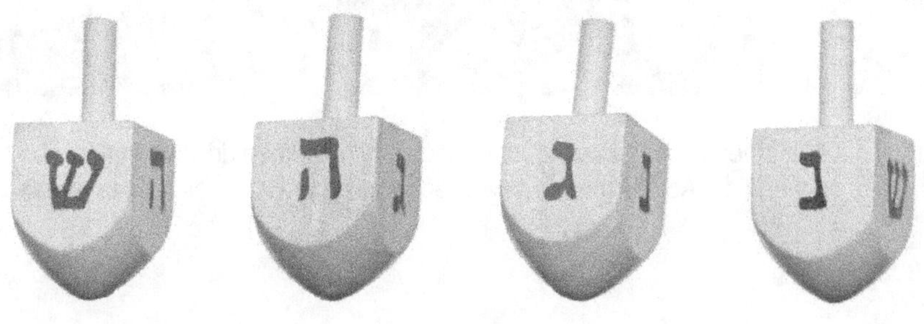

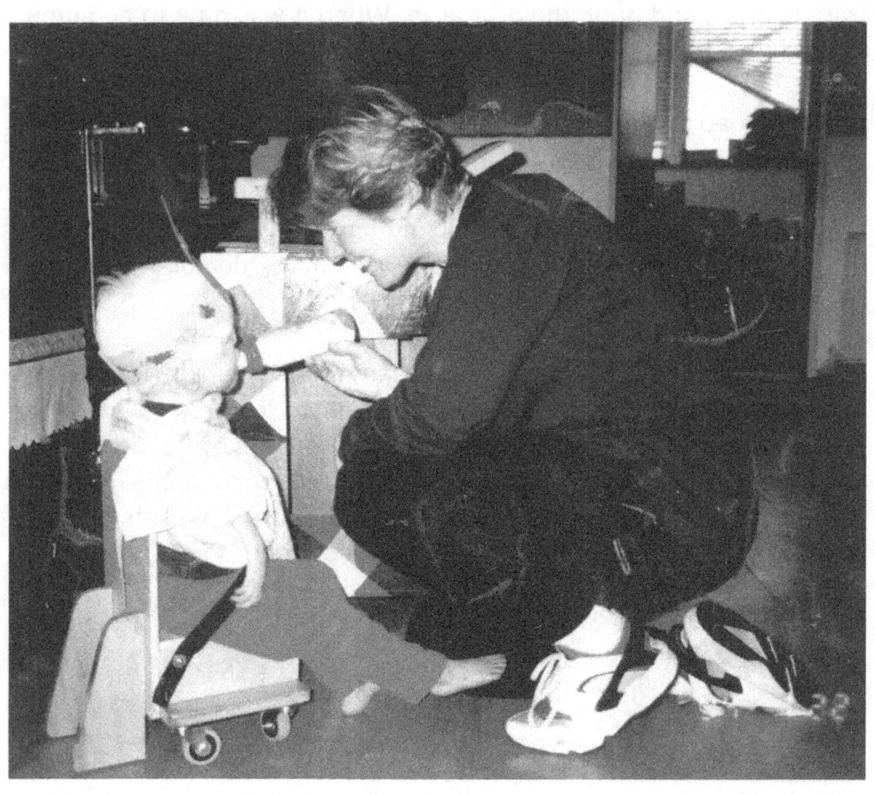

Na'il never learned to eat normal food. He didn't mind to keep drinking from his bottle, and neither did I. At least now I knew exactly how many calories his intake was.

7

"Weeping may endure for a night but joy comes in the morning!"
Psalm 30:5

Around the end of January 2000, the sleet gradually changed into heavy snow.

The next morning, we woke up to find another winter wonderland - Jerusalem was covered with a thick (30-40 cm) blanket and, because of broken tree branches, we literally had to saw our way to the street.

Na'il kept begging us to go outside, so Wim and I took turns carrying him in a baby seat on our back. The other children preferred to stay warm and dry at home ~ it would have been impossible for them to trudge through the heavy snow. Two days later, the melting snow turned to ice, which made walking even more hazardous.

Na'il's previous hearing test had been rather traumatic for him. Thanks to the blinking lights they used in Hadassah hospital, the new test turned out to be real fun.

"Na'il only has a small hearing-rest," the technician said. "That's probably the reason he constantly tries to wriggle out his hearing-aids. Come back in a few months' time and then we'll decide how to continue – with or without hearing aids."

It was a busy time with lots of doctor's visits. Na'il gradually began to enjoy them, especially the dentist! Arriving early, the little boy had the time of his life racing through the long corridors in his scooter; he followed each white coat, checked every open door and thought that also the staircase was a worthwhile area to investigate. Finally, it was his turn to enter the spacious treatment facility.

"Shalom Na'il!" someone welcomed him.

"Oh, how you've grown!" another exclaimed.

"My, how much he has changed!" his dentist remarked. They couldn't get over his developmental growth. Lying in the dentist chair, Na'il liked the big lamp well enough, but not the cleaning of his teeth.

"Na'il won't need further treatment under full anesthetics," Shabtai, his appointed dentist, informed me. "Next time laughing gas —nitro for short, will be sufficient."

Even though we were not Jewish, and didn't have to 'spring-clean' our house, Pesach was always a busy time. Having the children at home for the week-long holiday meant added stress when I had to prepare the Seder meal. Wim suggested to give me a break and we celebrate the Seder elsewhere. In a conference center near Bethlehem, we celebrated the Jewish Exodus from Egypt with about fifty Christians. We

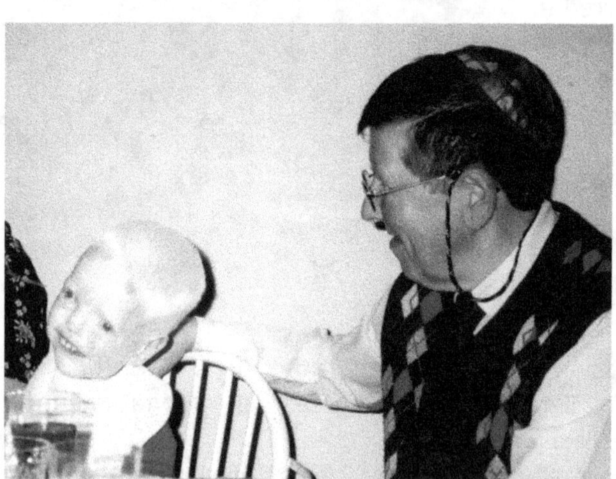

thought Na'il was 'safe' in the long corridors, until a loud noise reverberated through the stone building.

Lining the walls were three-meter-long wooden benches, and Na'il, seated on his scooter, decided to 'rearrange' them.

"So much for having a 'quiet' evening off," I muttered and joined our mischievous boy in the corridor.

Each time a virus was making its round, it seemed Na'il got it too. The May virus hit him hard, and he had been vomiting for a whole day. Worried, because he was unable to keep any formula down, I took him to Alyn hospital.

The pediatrician pinched his skin, immediately hooked him to an IV and kept him overnight. The next morning Na'il was confused to find Shula and her aid standing next to his bed. With his leg, he pushed Shula away – he wanted to stay in bed with his IV - that was much more fun! After one day at home to recuperate, Na'il was ready to go back to school.

We were blessed with the help of Joke, a Dutch volunteer. She took Na'il for walks and when necessary helped us around the house. One afternoon, Joke and I drove to Alyn to pick up Na'il. Rounding a corner we stopped in our tracks. The children were lined up in their car seats, waiting for the drivers to bring them home. Na'il sat next to a child who had dropped his lemonade bottle. Open-mouthed we watched how Na'il (strapped in his car seat), with great difficulty pushed himself to the center of the corridor, turned around and grabbed the bottle between his feet. Holding the bottle up-side-down he first checked what was in it, and then 'handed' the boy his bottle. With renewed effort, he pushed himself back against the wall. I had tears in my eyes when I hugged my precious little boy.

"Oh, he does that all the time," Shula later told me. "Na'il always helps his classmates - without being asked."

He just did it, as if it was the most logical thing to do. One day Na'il was in the kitchen while I prepared the dog's food. He opened the trash can with his foot for me to discard the tin.

Another school year was coming to an end and we celebrated Na'il's last school party in Alyn. He had to go to another school, but the problem was that nobody knew which one yet.

"Don't worry," the social worker said, "we have plenty of time till the end of August." She paused. "It has to be a school willing to accept a mentally and physically handicapped deaf child."

"Retarded?" I protested. "Na'il's a very bright child!"

The social worker explained that besides having little communicational skills, Na'il usually did what he wanted. That kind of behavior fell in the 'retarded' category. It was difficult to accept, but in my heart I knew the lady was right.

In special education, six of the eight weeks' summer holiday school continued to give children their much needed treatment.

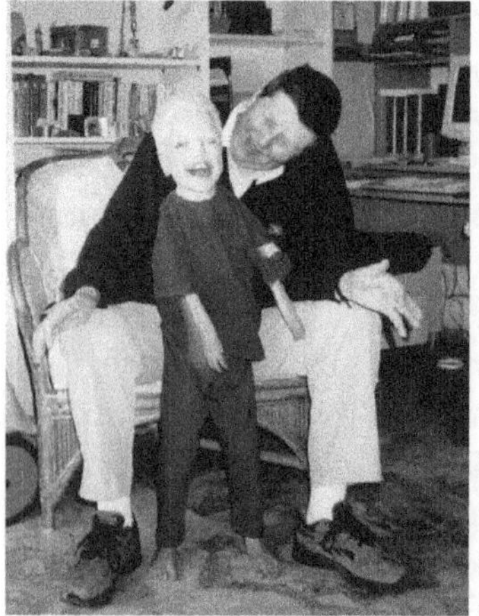

One day, Na'il showed off what he had learned in school: he walked, independently, for at least seven meters! He just couldn't stop walking from Wim to me and vice versa. Smiling triumphantly and trusting we would catch him, he let himself crash into our outstretched arms. Lacking shoulders to give him balance, it was

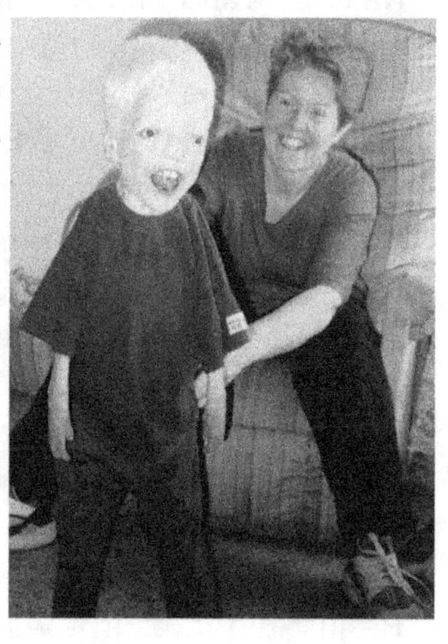

frightening to see him walk. But he did it! Again!

Like so many other 'impossible' things. Later, the physiotherapist told us that Na'il taught himself to walk on the ramp in the swimming pool.

Our upcoming trip to Holland had to be cancelled because Fahima needed an urgent eye operation. The usual 'hospital-mode' routine meant I stayed with Fahima during the day, and Wim took Na'il and Nadia to visit the patient. We'd always drink a cup of coffee together, after which I took the two children home with me again. (Moshiko's behavioral problems had been getting out of hand. To give us some breathing space, social services arranged for Moshiko to stay elsewhere during that summer.)

Jerusalem staggered under a blistering heat wave, which drained everyone's energy. Thankfully, the eye-department's air-conditioning kept things cool.

Na'il loved to play on Fahima's hospital bed and without taking any risks, was always careful to slide off. However, he must have miscalculated, for he fell on his bottom and from his reactions I knew it hurt him terribly. Afraid he had broken his tailbone, I took him to the Emergency department. The X-ray didn't show any fractures, but to be on the safe side, the doctor wanted to keep Na'il overnight - something we had not planned for at all! Thanks to the goodwill from the eye-department staff, Nadia could sleep over on the ward as well. Na'il and I spent the night on the children's ward.

The next morning, our little boy was as healthy as could be. I collected Nadia and we returned home. Especially for Na'il it had been a very exciting weekend!

The first of September loomed, and we still had no school for Na'il. But we kept hoping and praying something would be found at the last moment. Exhausted from the emotional stress we endured during the summer months, I longed for some 'peace and quiet' once the children returned to school.

Friday, September 1st. A very sad little boy watched the other children go back to their different schools. We couldn't explain it to him, and my heart broke to see him so sad.

Monday. My idea of taking Na'il to the Biblical Zoo to give him some fun didn't help - he was miserable.

Tuesday. I began my 'school offensive' - called people, faxed, and began to complain - something new for me. "This is going too far! The child needs to go to school, like all other children. What's going on here?"

Wednesday. Up in arms, I took Na'il to the City Hall's Educational department. The people were very sympathetic and agreed that something had to be done.

"Why don't you try Ma'ayan, St. Vincent," one of the ladies suggested. "For the time being, I think he should be able to stay in the Alyn School."

Filled with hope, I called the school principle. "I have to discuss it with the parents' committee first," she said. "I will call you on Sunday."

I wasn't sure if I could wait that long.

"Do you have season tickets here?" a nurse asked when she saw me enter Hadassah Hospital. At least, Na'il enjoyed his visit to the eye doctor that Thursday. He loved everything - the lights, the machines, the doctor! Even though he has white hair, a sign of albinism, the test showed that his eyes were normal.

"See you next year!" The doctor laughed.

"You can count on us, doctor!"

Full of hope I waited for Sunday's phone call and was devastated when the principle told me Na'il was NOT welcome to return to the Alyn School. Not even temporarily. I was getting desperate, and so was Na'il, who began to show signs of depression.

The social worker from Alyn came up with a few (belated) ideas, which we were going to check out the next day. The first school on the list seemed nice enough, the staff very sweet, but we felt Na'il's progress would suffer if he went there. The next one was an anthroposophical school. Not our favorite choice, but we decided to take a look anyhow. The school staff seemed to handle the very handicapped children in the class well. *Is this going to be the school for Na'il?* I wondered. My heart fell.

"What about the Ma'ayan School?" I whispered to the social worker.

"No! Na'il's a bright child. He's too good for that school!" She brushed City Hall's suggestion aside. "That's a school for hopeless cases!"

It seemed we didn't have a choice, and with heavy hearts agreed to try the anthroposophical school. But there was another catch.

"We'd love to have Na'il," the headmistress said, "but City Hall has to grant us an extra helper. Na'il needs special care." She promised to call us when they received an answer.

I felt frustrated, and seeing Na'il suffer emotionally made me more and more anxious. He had become the victim of bad planning and bureaucracy.

Na'il's front tooth, a crown, had fallen out, so I took him to the dentist. At least it was something I could do to make him happy! But after two hours in his favorite place, we had to go back home, back to the gloom and depression of not knowing when this nightmare would end.

Na'il not only needed friends and other children to be around, but structured days as well. I lacked the energy to take him shopping, or to do 'fun' things that eventually for him weren't fun at all. He wanted to go to school!

> ***"The only light at the end of the tunnel***
> ***is the light of the oncoming train...."***

"I'm very sorry, but we didn't get permission for an extra helper in the class," the anthroposophical teacher told me over the phone. Another closed door. My heart sank.

Our social worker tried to lift my spirits with the news that next week, an 'expert' would visit City Hall. Surely that lady would know how to deal with 'difficult' cases like Na'il....

Having to wait another endless week without any hope to cling too, was the straw that broke the camel's back - in this case mine. When I called Wim to tell him the bad news I began to cry and couldn't stop.

Shocked to hear me in such a state, he came home and took two weeks' holiday to help me with Na'il. Emotionally, I just couldn't take it anymore. The tension and stress of the summer months, together with the pain of seeing a six-year-old boy wake up depressed because he couldn't go to school - it just tore me apart.

September 24. The 'expert' called.

"Have you heard about St. Vincent and their Ma'ayan school?!" Wasn't that the same school the social worker thought Na'il was too good for?

By now we were ready to try anything, and I made an appointment for the next day.

The stately old building in Ein Kerem, dating from 1880, belonged to the Daughters of Charity of St. Vincent de Paul.

Since 1964 it had become the home of some seventy severely physically and mentally children. *Maon* (residence, home) St. Vincent also had a special education school on the premises which was called *Ma'ayan.* I looked around me, soaked in the peace and quiet, heard the birds singing their hearts out in the beautiful trees surrounding the building and knew in my heart, this is the place!

At first, Jacky, the headmistress, also thought Na'il was too good for the special education school they had on the premises. We never knew why she changed her mind, but when she said yes, I burst into tears.

"What's the matter?" she asked, shocked.

"It's just from joy and relief," I sniffed.

Jacky showed us around the building and we met several teachers and their helpers.

To think that in late August, this school had been suggested! The thought made me angry. Na'il had suffered terribly (and we with him!) only because of the terrible stigma attached to this institution ("hopeless" cases). And all this time, the answer had been right before our noses.

"When can he come?" I asked Jacky, hoping she would say tomorrow.

"I think it's better for him to start after the Jewish New Year," she said.

It meant another week at home. But what an enormous difference HOPE made.

That first morning in Ora's class, I stayed in the background to see how it went. After a few hours, Na'il felt so at home that the teacher told me I could go home. It was a comfort to leave Na'il in the capable hands of this confident, no-nonsense teacher.
It's hard to explain the feeling of elation I experienced while driving home to enjoy a cup of coffee in peace and quiet! It had been so long that I had almost forgotten how it felt.

That afternoon, the school bus brought home a completely changed boy ~ happy, satisfied, and smiling from ear to ear. Such a blessing!

Many years later, one of the teachers told me about the first time she had seen us. Stepping 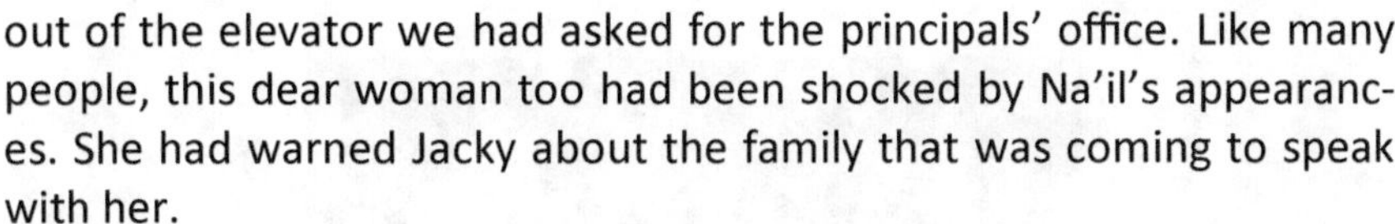 out of the elevator we had asked for the principals' office. Like many people, this dear woman too had been shocked by Na'il's appearances. She had warned Jacky about the family that was coming to speak with her.
However, when this teacher saw Na'il again on his first school day in Ma'ayan, she wondered why she had felt such a shock that day. All she saw was a beautiful, precious little boy!
It often happened this way - after the initial shock, people with great hearts saw Na'il's precious soul behind his handicap.
Unfortunately, there were also those who openly showed their disgust or terror. Children sometimes even called him an 'alien'. Then we were grateful Na'il could not hear their hurtful remarks.

A few days later it was *Yom Kippur* - Day of Atonement. It confused Na'il, and I felt frustrated for being unable to explain it to him.
But when he realized this was only a temporary break, that he really was going back to school, the smile didn't leave his face.

He returned to his class of seven children, one teacher and three to four aids. They had a so-called "*snoezel* room" (Dutch invention) which quickly became Na'il's favorite place! His classmates were rather passive and wheelchair bound, but our inquisitive boy preferred to roam around. Soon, Na'il's picture was taped on all school doors, with the warning, "Keep door shut!" He needed to learn discipline, which kept the teachers on their toes, but they loved it! Each day, Ora wrote another accomplishment in Na'il's notebook.

We couldn't stop thanking God for the gift of this wonderful school.

One day we drove past Alyn Hospital and I wondered about Na'il's reaction. To my amazement, on purpose he looked the other way and seemed relieved when we didn't turn into the driveway.

The fact that Na'il left the house with joy and returned satisfied and happy, to me was proof that it was the best place he could ever be!

So much for 'hopeless' cases, I thought.

Because of Na'il's successful enrolment in the *Ma'ayan* school, Alyn began to send more children there.

God's ways are always the best!

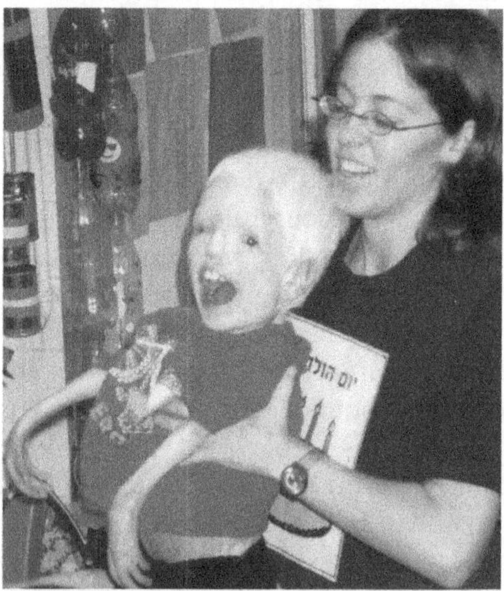

Ora, Na'il's teacher did an amazing job with Na'il!

8

A 'Re-born' Child

It was the beginning of 2001 and we had not heard from Na'il's parents for over six months. Then one day they called Kassem, the Social worker responsible for the family, asking why they were not allowed to see their child?!? Fortunately, Kassem persuaded them not to take Na'il for two nights, and called us to set a date. (It always had to be arranged in this roundabout way.)

Friday afternoon, January 12 we handed our little boy over to people who had become complete strangers to him. I fretted and worried, and with good reason - the next day Na'il returned in a state of shock. "Na'il cried non-stop," Mahmud told us. "He also refused to eat (drink). How on earth do you know what he means or wants?"

At home I took Na'il on my lap in the rocking chair and rocked him for half an hour. It took a few hours before he began to 'thaw'.

Sarah, our social worker at City Hall, (at one point we had four different social workers —one for each child), agreed that something had to be done! "This won't happen again," she vowed. "I'm going to speak with Kassem."

Jews, Arabs and Christians worked side by side in the *Ma'ayan* School. The Arab workers were angry when they heard about the traumatic meeting. "It would have been better for Na'il if his biological parents forgot all about him," one of the workers said. "A pity you didn't get him straight after he was born."

Because of the children's constant needs and care, Wim and I never had the opportunity to go away for a weekend. On Wim's birthday, January 19, for the first time in all those years, we took a 26-hour 'holiday' at a moshav near Jerusalem. Joke looked after Na'il and the dogs while the girls stayed with another friend. Only because Na'il knew and accepted Joke did we dare to give it a try. The children had a wonderful time. So did we!

I waited in City Hall for Mahmud and Sameera to join me for a meeting about Na'il, but they never showed up. Like any proud mother, I always took a stack of pictures of our little boy, and enthusiastically told Kassem about Na'il's antics.

"Kassem's blind," Sara whispered.

"Oh, I'm so sorry, Kassem!" I was grateful he couldn't see my embarrassed blush.

During that meeting, it was agreed that once a month, on a Shabbat morning, Mahmud would pick up Na'il at a pre-arranged meeting place and bring him back around 5 p.m. That was the best solution for Na'il and I hoped his parents would accept this new arrangement.

It was the season for doctor's visits.

Lying on the table in the neurologist's room Na'il had the time of his life ~ he jumped up and down with joy! The doctor fetched a colleague to look at Na'il.

"I've only read about these syndromes (Klein-Waardenburg) in the medical books," the doctor said. "Never seem them in real life. Very interesting."

Both Jews and Muslims circumcise their sons, but Na'il had been too weak to undergo this ritual. Mahmud wanted his son to be circumcised, so we went to see a urologist. From this specialist, I learned that Na'il had spent the first two months of his life in hospital.

"When the baby was brought home, his parents treated him like a lump of meat. A hopeless case ~ better left to die," the doctor read from the medical file.

Stunned, I looked at Na'il –a miracle!

"It's impossible to circumcise Na'il," the urologist informed me and thankfully, Mahmud accepted the specialist's answer.

Because Na'il belonged to a different health fund, I had to embark on a search for other doctors and specialists than we used so far. Planning each doctor's visit became a frustrating, time consuming process. It was always a struggle to get the necessary permits.

The urologist wanted to be sure Na'il didn't have an extra pair of kidneys, thus our boy had to undergo an ultra-sound - another thing he LOVED! Most children already freaked out upon entering the dark room filled with machinery.

"Gggchchchc," Na'il said.

"Why does he make those sounds?" The technician asked.

"His way of expressing he's happy and enthusiastic," I explained.

The technician laughed even louder when he did the ultrasound. Na'il laughed and giggled and gurgled and was as happy as can be. We went home with the proof that he had the right number of vital organs, no extra ones!

One day, Wim sprained his ankle and had to use crutches.

"Gggchchchc!" Na'il exclaimed when he saw Wim hobbling around and immediately tried to pry them away from his father.

Confused, Na'il looked from his teacher to the school psychologist when they visited our house. Ora, Na'il's teacher, told us that the staff continuously tried to find ways to teach him. We blessed them for their efforts! As we were talking about his development, it suddenly dawned upon me that the day Na'il came to live with us, in a way he had been reborn.

Judging from his present behavior and development, he acted like a 3-4-year-old - the years he lived with us. We were so grateful to God for the many wonderful changes Na'il had gone through. Even after a few months in the *Ma'ayan* school!

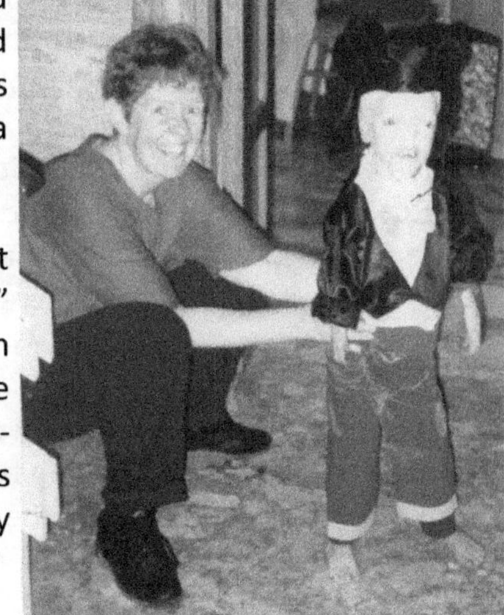

"We'll have a Purim party at school. Would you like to join us?" Ora wrote in Na'il's communication notebook. Who wouldn't? In the 'old' days I used to make the children's Purim costumes myself. This time I bought a nice little Mickey Mouse costume that Na'il loved.

"There is no group of people more full of fun than those with severe handicaps who have accepted themselves and others just as they are." **Nancy Doyle, from the book *Children of Grace*.**

The same was true about people working with special needs children! Everyone had so much fun, and I didn't know who enjoyed themselves more - the children or the staff!

My eighty-year-old Mom still lived independently in Amsterdam, Holland, but Parkinson disease began to debilitate her everyday life. Added to that, she was lonely and didn't get enough help. I worried about her. Why not ask her to come live with us? suddenly popped into my mind. "What do you think, Wim?" I asked him.

He didn't have to think long. "The Bible clearly says we should look after the widows and orphans," he reminded me.

My two sisters (one lived in Holland, the other in Sweden) were open to the idea of Mom coming to live with us. But how to convince Mom? I thought.

"I'll hand-deliver your invitation to Mom," my sister suggested.

I expected Mom would need at least six months to get used to the idea, but when the Lord prepares someone's heart, you just must take the first step and the rest will follow.

Mom had tears in her eyes when she finished reading the letter.

"When would you like to go to Israel, Mom?" my sister asked.

"As soon as possible!" she replied.

When I told the children about *Savta* (Grandmother) coming to live with us, they were enthusiastic. I quickly began to prepare the house for *Savta's* arrival. Because we didn't have a spare bedroom, in the spacious living room we created a small room behind a row of bookcases.

God not only took care of elderly people, but canaries as well - Mom found a good home for her little bird.
From delivering the letter to the implementation of the plan took only three weeks!

It was an emotional time. Moshiko's behavioral problems had been deteriorating to such extent, that he had to be placed out of the house. Preparing for *Savta's* arrival was balm on my wounded soul and gave me something positive and happy to think about.

I flew to Holland on April 1 and two days later, Mom and I returned to Israel. The children warmly welcomed their *Savta.* She was tired after the long and emotional trip, and sat down in an easy chair. I don't think Na'il remembered his grandmother from our previous visit, many years ago, but he went over to her and managed to 'climb' on her lap.

With tears in my eyes I watched the two of them - kindred spirits who instantly found a way to each other's heart.

9

""Oh, that you would bless me and enlarge my territory! Let your hand be with me...." And God granted his request."

When Wim and I got married in 1979 not many people had heard about the 'Prayer of Jabez' in 1 Chronicles 4:10. It was our wedding text.

Not far from where we lived was a beautiful hilly, rocky area filled with wild flowers. I loved to take the dogs there because they could roam around freely, and it saddened me to see how the beautiful area gradually had to make way for villas!

We had seen the house being built - from the strong foundations upward until it was finished. It struck me how different it was from the other villas in the neighbourhood. This house wasn't four stories high, including many steps, but was built horizontally and had a ramp leading from the sidewalk to the front door. That would be a wonderful house for us, I thought, but immediately discarded the idea. People build these houses for themselves, not to rent them out.

And then one day, a sign appeared: For Rent.

Already for months I had this 'inkling', a feeling that change was in the air but knew it wasn't connected to Moshiko's departure and Savta's entry into our family. As time went by, our present house had become unsuitable due to the changing needs of the children. It became more difficult for the girls to climb the stairs to their bedrooms and getting in and out of the bathtub to take a shower. When Savta went for a walk, I first had to carry the walker down several steps. The ground floor toilet could only be reached by using the stairs as well.

It was obvious we needed to move, but I didn't have the energy to go house hunting. And where in Jerusalem would we be able to find a suitable and affordable place?

"That villa is way too expensive," I told Wim. "We can never afford it." Lord, You know the kind of house we need for our special needs children and Savta, I thought, and decided to trust Him to lead us to it.

Which He did. It happened to be right in front of our eyes - 200 meters from where we lived! The villa for rent!

Around the end of June, Micha, the owner showed us around the house, and three weeks later we signed a 4-year contract, with an option for extension.

"I hope the house will be ready around the end of August," Micha said.

I immediately started packing while dreaming about the spacious 7-room house!

Summer was always a time of viruses and one-day bugs. That summer our family was hit with a vengeance. Fahima passed it on to me, and then Na'il too began to vomit. When he continued throughout the afternoon, I worriedly took him to Hadassah's emergency department - his 'favourite' place. The dehydrated child was immediately hooked to an IV and had to stay overnight. Slumped in an uncomfortable chair next to his bed, I tried to get some sleep. The next morning Na'il was discharged, but it almost took a week before he was his 'old' self again.

Our little sunshine! Everyone who knew the boy couldn't help but love him! He was such a special child! The little 'scooter' continued to be his main means of moving around, without the use of the safety belt — he now could stand up and walk. Unsupported, legs wide apart and amidst peals of laughter and ecstasy, Na'il continued to 'practice'. At school, he was making good progress too, and 'liked' the speech therapist who taught him how to use his communication board.

Na'il either liked or didn't like people (e.g. he openly disliked his biological mother) and once his mind was made up, that was it. Neither could you force him to do something he didn't want. Talking about stubborn/strong willed! But thanks to this trait, he managed to overcome seemingly insurmountable obstacles. Without whining, crying or temper tantrums, he thought about it, observed the 'problem' and then tackled it.

10

A New Page

The previous house had been old, dark and for me was tainted with many unpleasant and traumatic memories. The new house was light, spacious and completely new.
Even though the house was not yet finished, we moved on August 30. It felt as if a new page of our lives began; my heart expanded within my chest, it was as if I could breathe easier. Such a difference! With renewed energy, we set out to tackle the enormous job of getting the house ready before school started, September 1.

Already during those first days, many seemingly 'small' things turned out to be a great blessing. The first one was the bathroom on the ground floor. We even had two – one with a bath, the other with a spacious shower cabin. Na'il's love affair with the bathtub was an on-going thing, and each day he would spend at least an hour there. Now I could easily keep an eye on Na'il without having to race up and down the stairs each time I heard a 'suspicious' noise.
The other blessing was a time-saving one. Because of the distance from the house to the road, the children needed at least 15 minutes to get there. Then we'd have to wait for the school bus to pick them up. Now, the driver honked his horn, and the children went from the house into the school bus. Because I was never sure what time they returned home, I often had to wait at least 15-30 minutes, rain or shine, to collect them, using the time to catch up with my reading. Now I either saw the school bus turning into the street, or heard them honk. It made life so much easier!

The appointment had been made months ago, and even though I couldn't spare the time, I took Na'il to the orthopedic surgeon at his health fund clinic.

"Sorry, but I only treat adult patients," the surgeon said when it finally was our turn.

"Why didn't they tell me?" I complained to the secretary.
The woman shrugged and gave me a new appointment for the children's surgeon.
A week later we were back. While waiting for our turn, Na'il had the time of his life watching children exciting the plaster room - screaming. He became the star of the waiting room and everyone was very nice to him, which blessed me tremendously.

"What are you doing here?" Dr. Joseph, our orthopedic surgeon from Alyn peered over his glasses. "I don't want to see you here. Why not in Alyn?"
After I told him about the health-fund headaches, he immediately wrote a letter. "Here. This will do. See you in Alyn. Bye!"
Na'il was upset the doctor didn't even look him over....

We had moved into a house that was far from finished, and the first few months were hectic with workers coming and going. Someone had to fix the kitchen, or the plumbing, or put glass in the frames of our upstairs bedroom, or fix the stairs. There were times I had to run up and down between three different experts asking me questions or who wanted to show me something – all at the same time....
Na'il loved all the activity and even tried to 'help' some of the workmen, who were all very nice to him.

The high holidays were long and boring for Na'il. He filled his days by practicing his walking, and gave us many a fright by letting himself fall backwards on his scooter.

We celebrated *Rosh haShana,* the Jewish New Year with a festive meal and before we knew it, it was time to build a Succa on the balcony during the Feast of Tabernacles. Na'il loved to sit in it and just look around.

Dr. Sheffer, the genetics doctor in charge of the children's development clinic at the Leumit health fund, had seen Na'il after he was born. The woman couldn't believe her eyes when we entered her office. Even though the waiting room was filled to overflowing, she spent an hour with us.

I asked her the question which seemed to be at the forefront of many people's minds when they saw Na'il: What is his life expectancy?

"People with these syndromes have normal life expectancies," she told me. "But, later in life, emotionally it will become very challenging for Na'il. It isn't easy to grow up with such a complex handicap."
I decided not to dwell on 'later' and trust God to give us the wisdom and grace to deal with it when the time came.

Na'il's cheek was swollen, and even though I couldn't see anything, we went to Hadassah's dental walk-in clinic. Again, staff and dentists couldn't believe the change in Na'il. He was the star of the ward, walking in and out the different treatment rooms, smiling happily and enjoying himself tremendously. A dentist checked him and didn't find anything wrong. "I guess it's a new tooth breaking through," he said.
After having dropped Na'il at school, I just arrived home when Ora called. "He fell asleep in class. I think he's really ill."

"So much for some 'peace and quiet'," I mumbled under my breath and drove back to school.
The next day I could see he wasn't feeling well, and got worried when he went back to bed by himself. Something was wrong, but what could it be? I kept him home to observe the symptoms, which were strange because he didn't have a fever. However, as the day progressed, he became more and more lethargic.
The next day I was back at the dentist in Hadassah Hospital. One of the professors noticed a tiny necrotic wound - probably from sticking pieces of broken umbrellas in his mouth when I wasn't looking. The dentist cleaned the wound with pure oxygen, gave a prescription for antibiotics and by the time we returned home Na'il was already feeling 90% better. Thank God we found the reason for his mysterious illness!

Everything connected with water held a great attraction for Na'il. The first rain wasn't an exception. Because of the long, dry summer months, in Israel the first rain (*Yoreh*) is always a reason to rejoice. Hard to imagine when you live in a country that is has rain throughout the year, but not in Israel. Even after having become soaking wet from a downpour, people still called it a blessing, good for the country.

The Kinneret (Sea of Galilee) had to be filled up again – it was where Israel got its drinking water!

Noticing it had begun to rain, I took Na'il outside and through sign language explained what was happening. I deeply inhaled, telling him to smell the rain – petrichor. In the end, I had to drag him inside, because he would have loved to stay there.

School was a place Na'il learned many new things. One of them was potty training. He still wore diapers, and even though he went to the toilet for bowel move-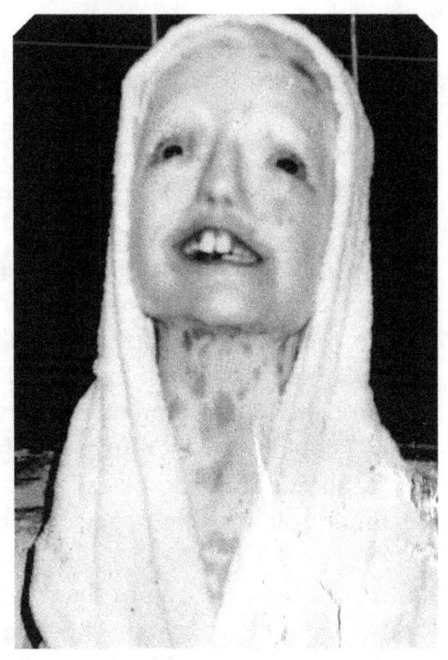ments, Ora wanted to wean him off diapers. But Na'il thought that urinating on the floor was much more fun - then he could play with it with his feet…. What he didn't count on was that the floor became slippery - he made a split and fell. Ora called to tell me what happened. "I don't think he has broken something," she added.

That afternoon, I followed Na'il's usual routine – first the toilet, then his bottle, then the bathtub. I could see that he was in pain. That's logical, after a split. Probably strained muscles, I reasoned. Better keep him home tomorrow, and rest.

But after two days there wasn't much improvement and Na'il refused to stand on his left leg. Worried, I took him to his orthopedic surgeon, Dr. Joseph in Alyn. The x-ray showed Na'il had broken the neck of his femur! I felt terrible! Which mother lets her child suffer from an un-treated fracture for two days? I berated myself.

According to Dr. Joseph, this was a difficult fracture to treat; the only thing he could do was immobilize the leg with elastic bandages. Home again, Na'il became more and more restless and then began to moan softly.

We arrived at Hadassah's emergency department at 6 p.m. The waiting game began. The surgeon had to run between the emergency department and the operation theatre and it seemed ages before he could see us. Most of the night I slept on a mattress on the floor until they finally arranged a bed on the children's ward.

Being 'only' foster parents, not legal guardians, we were not allowed to sign consent forms or for a hospitalization. Mahmud brought his whole family to the hospital. Na'il was in great pain, and I cringed when Sameera touched his painful limb.
Doesn't she understand he doesn't want to be touched? I thought irritably. I couldn't tell her, because she spoke only Arabic.
    "Mahmud, can you please explain to Sameera this doesn't help?"
Mahmud told his wife to back off.

In Israeli hospitals, one of the parents must stay with the sick child, 24 hours a day. Part of our "hospitalization mode" was that Wim took over from me in the evenings so I could go home and get some sleep. I wasn't home long when Wim called. "Na'il is becoming more and more restless," he said.
Truth to be told, so was I. I felt terrible, not knowing how he was - I wanted to be with my little boy. We decided it would be better for all of us that I returned to the hospital and stay with Na'il for the duration of the hospitalization. On the one hand, it was tiresome, but having to race between the hospital and home was too much for me.

While waiting for things to happen on the ward, I had many interesting talks with family members of other sick children and medical staff. Everyone was curious about the little boy with the white hair. Some parents responded with shock and rejection, others were curious but, in a nosy, negative way. Most however, were positive and sweet. Mothers listened when I told them the story of our lives, and literally, thanked God for the work we did with these special children. A grandmother blessed me by looking past Na'il's strange features and seeing the beauty of the child within. Those reactions were balm for my exhausted soul.

Friday afternoon a religious man entered the room Na'il shared with another child. "May you be blessed with good health and a Shabbat Shalom!"

"Would you like a sandwich or a warm meal?" a volunteer from a religious organization asked. "It's free."

"*Todah rabah*! Thank you very much!" I gratefully accepted the sandwich.

"Mothers of sick children have to eat too!" the woman said and went to the next parent.

The surgical children's ward on the 4th floor was a place where I saw Jewish and Arab doctors work alongside Jewish and Arab nurses, to give Jewish and Arab patients, lying side by side, the best medical care possible. You didn't hear that on the news!

Shabbat arrived and Na'il was in the best of moods, especially when I put him in his buggy to watch the children parading in the corridor holding their IV's. He was crazy about them. Not the children, the IV's!

"We have to postpone Na'il's operation," the orthopedic surgeon informed me. "Because of the rain, there have been so many traffic accidents that we have hardly time to breathe."

Sunday, October 28, Na'il fasted from noon onwards - the Spica cast was to be administered under full anesthetics. An auxiliary nurse took us down to the operating rooms; wearing a special outfit, including a hair covering and face mask, I carefully lifted Na'il onto the operating table. He looked at all the machines and lights and became very excited! The anesthetist put the mask on his face for the first anesthesia. Na'il deeply inhaled the first whiffs and was 'hooked' from that moment on....

When he awoke in the recovery room he immediately accepted his new harness! Obviously now without pain, he was as happy as could be! On Monday morning, we visited the plaster room for some adjustments to the Spica cast. Children usually screamed when they saw the frightening place with the electric saw. Na'il was so excited that I had a hard time keeping him to lie still on the x-ray table.

Even more exciting was the CT scan the next day! Never before had the staff experienced a child who behaved like Na'il - it was hilarious! The fractured bone was in the right position and we finally could go home. Children's Surgery on the 4th floor had become his most favorite place!

For his (and my) peace of mind, I didn't want Na'il to stay home for 5 weeks – the time he had to wear the Spica cast. I rented a special Spica cast car seat so he could safely travel to school. Because Na'il was not allowed to take a bath, we had to find other ways to keep him occupied. I had been rather worried about that, but in the end, that had not been necessary. Our little boy was happy watching his favorite videos. We didn't hear a peep or a grunt or a complaint – nothing. He accepted his lot, and that was it.

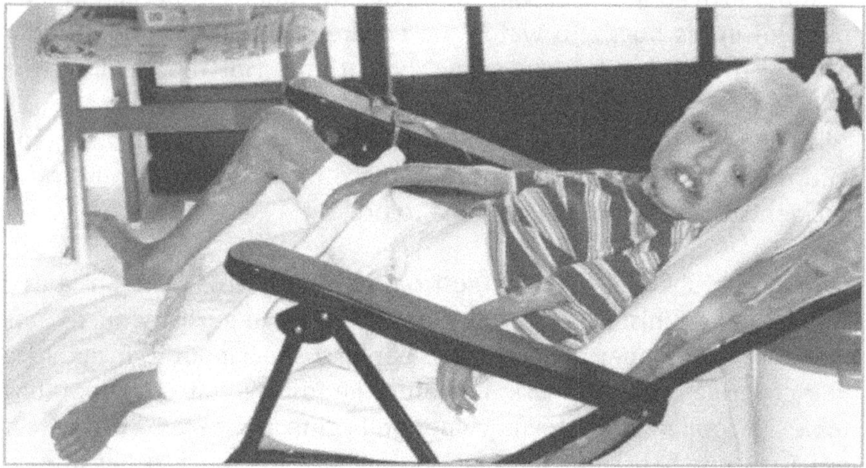

Around 7 p.m., we carried Na'il upstairs to his bed. In order to prevent pressure sores we had to turn him every two hours; he hardly noticed it when we changed his position in the middle of the night. It was quite a challenge to keep his skin intact. Because of the baby formula, Na'il's stools were very soft and it couldn't be prevented that some got under the plaster. Those were heavy, tiring weeks with broken nights, but Na'il was an easy-going child, who accepted his mishap with a smile. That was such a blessing!

Usually, removing the plaster with an electric saw was so frightening that children needed to be sedated. Of course, Na'il LOVED it! Once freed from his harness, the first thing we could do was give him a good soak. That wasn't a luxury - he stank! Not only did the x-ray show that the fracture was healed, but also that Na'il had osteoporosis!
Na'il figured that since the cast was off, he instantly could walk again. I had a hard time restraining him from getting out of his buggy. He still had a long way to go and the school physiotherapist taught him how to slowly and gradually get his mobility back.

At home, he was zooming around in his scooter, the TV had lost its charm, and he was back to being bored. In other words, life had returned to normal!

In the middle of December Na'il had his half-yearly dental appointment. In order to have a parking place, I needed to be there early. It gave Na'il the opportunity to spend all his energy and enthusiasm beforehand. When it was his turn he was tired, and cooperated most of the time. He loved the chair and surroundings, but opening his mouth was another matter. The only way to treat him was by giving him nitro (laughing gas). After one such treatment he laughed and chortled the whole morning. Probably they had given him a bit too much, but now I understood why it was called 'laughing gas'.

Slowly, the year 2001 ended. Even though so many negative and difficult things had happened, we still had so much to be thankful for!
God had been good to us!

Petrichor ~ essence of Rock, is derived from the Greek words *Petros* (stone) and *Ichor* (fluid flowing in veins of gods). It means the pleasant smell of the first rain after a long period of warm dry weather. Two Australian researchers discovered that this fragrance is an oily essence that comes from rocks or soil that are often clay-based. It's a complicated set of at least 50 (!) different compounds, like a perfume. During dry spells, the vegetation gives off the oils, which is absorbed by the rock surface and soil particles. When the first rains begin, these fragrances are released into the air, and this is what we smell - *Petrichor.*

11

"Joy is NOT happiness.
In the Hebrew mind joy means the absolute assurance
that God has a plan, that He has not lost interest in my prob-
lems, nor has He lost the power to deal with them."
Randy Smith

Every year, I asked snow for my birthday. It seemed that in 2002 I was going to get my wish. The meteorologists predicted a possibility of 25 cm. of snow for the 7th of January. Eighty snow ploughs and crews were on stand-by, vehicles were equipped with snow chains and 4x4 jeeps stood ready to transport the sick and elderly. After school activities had been cancelled, and the moment the first real flakes appeared, the schools closed and children were sent home.

It's generally known that snow makes it impossible to drive in hilly Jerusalem, so most businesses closed earlier than usual too. The Jerusalem-Tel Aviv highway was closed for over three hours. Bus services halted by mid-afternoon, forcing many people to walk home in often unsuitable footwear; many neighborhoods were accessible only by foot. Cellular phones went dead and traffic lights failed. Police emergency hotlines were constantly busy, because the 'whole world' was calling. Passengers were stranded in the central bus station, and three buses trying to leave, found their way blocked by snow and had to reverse.

This was typical Jerusalem mayhem during a snow storm, and by the time buses were finally able to resume driving, rush hour traffic had been built up, creating even more chaos than usual.

We were grateful the whole family was safely home and that we could watch the winter wonderland from inside. It surely had been a memorable birthday! Na'il loved it when we took him for a walk through the snow. Later that evening we saw many people taking a stroll through the soft still night, and I spotted two jackals, hiding behind some bushes.

I didn't have to listen to the early morning radio broadcast at 6 a.m. to know if schools were to be open or not. During the night, the snow had turned into rain, dashing the children's hopes for another holiday. However, the weather man promised that another cold front was on the way! He was right, for a day later another 5-cm. snow fell. Subsequent rain soon turned everything into ice!

That spring, while nature bloomed its heart out, the country was torn to pieces by one terror attack after another. Israelis faced triple 'A' terror: Anywhere, Anytime, Anyone. Our Dutch family became increasingly worried by watching too much (biased) news. Despite everything, Savta still loved living in 'dangerous' Israel.

Like most Israelis, we tried to continue our lives as normal as possible. Each morning we prayed for wisdom and protection, open hearts to hear God's still voice in case of danger. We felt safe in His care.

Unlike Arab terrorists, Jews saw each life as precious and of inestimable value. The Talmud taught: "He who saves a single life, saves an entire universe."

"How is your 'project' doing?" Dr. Sheffer asked during our twice-yearly check-up, referring to Na'il. She called a colleague to see the 'wonder boy'. "This child is proof of what can be done with these special needs children, when they are in the right environment – a loving home!" she said.

Even though we had not been in contact with Mahmud for quite a long time, I hesitated to call him. What if Na'il visits his parents and suddenly the security situation changes? I shivered at the scenario of him being trapped in a closed-off village, unable to go back home. It was better to let things be.

Our birthday boy's school party was celebrated in full style with other classes and lots of staff members joining in the fun. There were songs, games, balloons, candles, presents, and a compilation of drawings made by the children for Na'il's 8th birthday. We were so touched by all the work and effort the staff had made to give these special children as much happiness as possible!

In order to find out how Na'il could best be taught, we were advised to undergo an expensive test in the Sha'arei Zedek hospital. Na'il was surprised to find his teacher Ora, the teacher's aide, and the speech therapist waiting for him. He clearly was at a loss as to what was going to happen. Neither did I for that matter. I fretted about his behavior and hoped he would be cooperative.

After observing the little boy for a while, two ladies tried different approaches. Na'il was neither interested nor enthusiastic, and with his foot kept pointing to the door – he wanted out! Only when the computer was turned on and he grasped the idea of the program, was he willing to sit and cooperate somewhat. The women were amazed by Na'il's charm.

"He is a strong-willed child, who needs to know his boundaries," they wrote in the report. I noticed he had been testing them all the time. In the scope of 15 minutes, they had seen his behavior change from baby to toddler, to curious older boy, then back to preschooler again. There were also wide gaps between his emotional and mental development. Because of the test, they could advise school what they should try to work on, and which areas should wait till a later stage. Na'il's communication book was to be expanded, and another one made to use at home, for which we were grateful. The ladies were also amazed by Na'il's capacity to make clear what he wanted.

We were aware of that, but it was nice that others noticed it too! This 1.02 cm. tall, 10 kg. blue-eyed bundle of life was a source of blessing and pride for us!

What we perceived as a 'disaster' became a welcome August activity for Na'il. Our upstairs balcony had to be repaired, but in order to know where the leaks were, we had to fill it with water. In the evenings, we put Na'il in the center of the balcony and let him play with the hose while the balcony filled up. Due to the extreme heat, the water evaporated quickly and Na'il couldn't wait to go upstairs.

That August was long, hot, tiring, very busy and filled with even more terrorist attacks and heartbreaks, which, like the heat waves, didn't seem to let up.

Due to several important doctors' appointments, we were not able to go on holiday. Added to the balcony headache we also had planned to purchase two air conditioners – finally.

I wrote a series of booklets about "Benny White", hoping that people would use it as a tool to teach healthy children about special needs children. Even though nobody was interested in buying the stories that were based on Na'il's life, it was fun creating them!

The national new school year, the 1st of September, began with the usual teachers' strikes. Thankfully, our children could begin school as usual, because Special Education rarely strikes.

Rosh haShana, the birthday of the world, of Creation, we celebrated with friends. It was to be our last holiday with Savta. Mom had been with us for 1½ years now, and we'd love to keep her with us but on a practical level it had become too complicated. Every six months Mom's visa needed to be renewed and she had to leave the country at least once a year. Due to the 'security situation', her medical insurance was causing problems – a big worry for me. Above all, Savta missed her age group, wanted to speak Dutch and the high summer temperatures were also hard for her.

In April, my sister had applied for a place for Mom in a Dutch senior citizens' home. We had seen God perform a miracle when Mom came to live with us. Anew, God did a miracle by providing a beautiful room for her, in record time! I accompanied Mom to Holland, helped her settle in and was back in Israel before the Feast of Tabernacles, Succot, began.

It was obvious that Na'il missed *Savta,* whom he loved very much. They had this special 'connection', and he often 'crawled' on her lap, all by himself, just to be with her. At least we had lots of pictures to remember those special times.

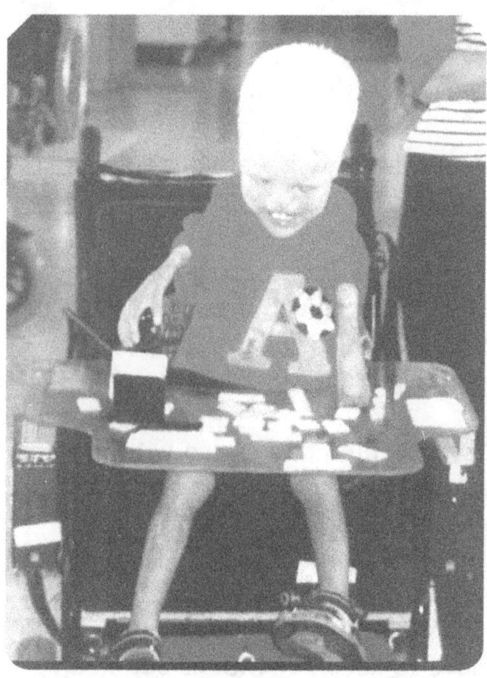

"Amazing! Unbelievable! A natural! A wonder boy!" The occupational therapist exclaimed when she gave Na'il a trial session in a motorized wheelchair. The chair was way too big for him, and the joystick had to be adjusted with Velcro, but the moment the power was turned on, Na'il was on his way.

Effortlessly he maneuvered himself through narrow doors, into the elevator, and the long corridors. Usually, children needed at least 1½ hours before they got used to the strange wheelchair. Na'il acted as if he had been driving these types of wheelchairs all his life! Stuck in the elevator, he got out in reverse, without bumping into the sides or blinking an eye. I was soooo proud of him! Na'il loved every minute of the 'lesson', and was disappointed it was over so quickly.

"You can apply for Na'il's own motorized wheelchair now." The occupational therapist was very pleased.

While Joke stayed home to look after the girls, we took Na'il on a 'holiday' to Yad haShmonah. He loved the wooden cabin, was crazy about the dining room and of course wanted to explore everything.

6 a.m. Shabbat morning, our little boy was ready for action! We never had a quiet moment, and no time to relax – the whole day we were on the go.

Wim and I were exhausted from pushing the buggy in the hilly area, while Na'il still had all this energy to spend.

"Let's take him to the pool," I suggested, "that will make him tired."

After 10 minutes in the 'cold' water, much cooler than the usual 33 degrees Celsius from the Alyn pool, Na'il looked blue and his teeth were chattering. He wanted OUT. Whatever we tried, he refused to go back in. So much for our good idea! It was to be our last 25-hour 'holiday'. We had tried, but Na'il couldn't cope being away from the two of us, not even when Joke looked. Taking him along wasn't much of a holiday.

"Life is easier than you think! All you have to do is…
Accept the impossible; do without the indispensable;
bear the intolerable and be able to smile at anything."

"He cannot be treated by the orthopedic surgeon in Alyn hospital," Na'il's health fund informed us. We had to return to the clinic in the center of town - always a time-consuming activity. Na'il didn't mind, he loved new clinics and buildings. Dr. Joseph looked at Na'il's spine. "He's developing a scoliosis (crooked spine)." My heart fell when I heard him mutter something about a brace. It would make Na'il less mobile.

The health clinic's eye doctor was another favorite we could add to Na'il's list. The perceptive child immediately noticed that there was an ultrasound room at the end of the corridor. Lacking the patience to wait for his turn, he set out to explore all the other rooms. Closed doors weren't a problem - he opened them with his mouth.

I constantly had to run after him, apologize to a surprised doctor and patient and quickly close the door. In the meantime, our inquisitive little guy got into all kinds of other mischief! He loved the place, especially when a nurse allowed him to stay in her room. Compared to all that fun, the check up was rather tame, although he did like the light the doctor shone into his eyes!

It had always been our dream to visit Eilat one day. Located at the southern tip of Israel, near the Red Sea, the distance (a five-hour drive from Jerusalem), and the need for lodgings made it impossible. Then one day, someone blessed the Embassy staff and their families with a long weekend in Eilat, all expenses paid. We thought we were dreaming when we saw the suite, which even included a Jacuzzi!

Na'il loved the Jacuzzi and the camping bed we brought along. For hours he played with a dolphin-shaped balloon. He was thrilled when we visited the underwater observatory, and even the long bus ride back to Jerusalem was exciting. We video-taped much of the weekend, and he watched the tape repeatedly.

Years later, he saw a picture of the Eilat Marina in a magazine. Smiling his glorious smile, he enthusiastically tapped with his toe on the hotel in the picture. He remembered!

That December was a month full of joy and blessings. Na'il's *Chanukah* party was a great success, and as usual, our little boy was the star of the show. I filmed the school party, and wrote a story about it, which you can read at the end of the chapter.

Maoz Tsur – Rock of Ages is the opening song for *Chanukah.* It was a fitting closure of a very difficult and traumatic year for the Jewish people.

Maoz Tsur

"Rock of Ages, let our song, praise thy saving power. Thou amidst the raging foes, wast our sheltering tower; Furious they assailed us, but thine arm availed us and thy word, broke their sword when our own strength failed us."

Chanukah in haMinzar

Locals call it *"haMinzar"*- the monastery, and associate it with hopeless cases. I'm looking forward to celebrating *Chanukah* with them. The guard waves at me as I maneuver the car in the courtyard. On the flat roof of the old building, surrounded by palm trees and cypresses, colorful sheets and towels are drying in the balmy December sun; shouts coming from the kitchen - situated under the building's main entrance - tell me Gabriella is bossing her co-workers again. I climb the stairs and zigzag through the labyrinth of corridors towards the main hall on the second floor.

A cacophony of sounds greets me as I enter the packed room.
"O, great you could make it, welcome!" Several people hug me. Devoted staff and wheelchair-bound children, their faces bright with anticipation, line the walls of the usually somber room, now decorated with colorful banners, streamers and lights.

Na'il, our severely disabled foster son, seems confused – am I taking him away from the fun? In Hebrew sign-language I explain that we're not going to see the doctor, but I'm here to film the party.
The music teacher strikes up a song, the adults join in and the party is on. Many of these children can't speak, but they understand the language of rhythm and music.
Swaying in their wheelchairs, some clumsily clapping their hands, they are delighted.

Each class represents a Chanukah theme; cardboard drawings, taped on the back of their chairs, picture a Dreidle, a candle, a torch, or a jug.
"They have been working on it for weeks on end," Jackie, the school's headmistress, says in a stage-whisper.
One class at a time, the children are wheeled around, contentment showing on their faces. We sing and clap for them. I'm not sure who is enjoying the party most, the staff or the children.
"Isn't it fantastic?" Sister Susan beams as she passes, trying to capture as much as possible on film.

Na'il's latest hobby is spitting out candles – a smart solution for his inability to blow. Someone released him from his chair, and he is on his way to show off his skill on the eight burning candles, each one secured in a sand-filled box. I force myself to stay put and leave him to Ora, his teacher.

"Not yet, mister!" She scoops up the boy - tiny and light for his eight years - and brings him back to his group, patiently waiting in their chairs. Na'il keeps the staff on their toes with his exploits. They love it.

His class -the jugs- parades while we sing the song "*kad katan*", little jug. Eliyahu, Na'il's favourite music teacher, treats him to a ride on his shoulders, and jigs him around. Na'il roars with laughter - the wilder the better- while I hold my breath till he's safely back on his feet again. "No, you can't run around now, savlanut, have patience!" Ora secures him in his chair.

Enters Yuval, the clown. His balloon tricks and funny antics cause the children's excitement to rise even more. Na'il is intrigued by the rubber chicken jumping out of a hat. Ora allows him to follow Yuval around.

"You want to dance?" the clown notices Na'il's rhythmic movements – he feels the loud music. Carefully, Yuval takes the little, claw-like hands and together they shuffle.
He couldn't have given the boy a bigger present.

"What is this?" the clown asks another child, while holding a monkey puppet.

"*Abba*! Daddy!" yells the exuberant boy. He beats a roll on the wheelchair's secured table, and bobs his head up and down.

The electric lights dim. Numerous candles brighten up the dark hall, as each class lights their Chanukiah. Na'il can't wait, this is his specialty.

"No, not yet, there's more to come." Rina, the teacher's aide, keeps him secure on her lap - at a safe distance from the burning candles - while around them sparklers appear. The children's faces glow from

wonder; each time it's a new and thrilling experience.
The candles make a sizzling sound when Rina permits Na'il to spit them out. Then he enjoys watching the smoldering stubs.
A boy tries to eat a jelly-filled *Sufganiyah*. Tenderly, Jackie wipes some of the donut's filling off his cheek. "Did you enjoy the party, my dear?"

"Aaaaahhh!" he answers with a widespread grin, flaps his hands wildly and sends his treat flying.

Outside, I savor the fresh air, the birdsong and peaceful quiet surrounding this place. Without encountering another car ascending the same steep, narrow, and winding road, I reach Mary's well. A group of tourists blocks my way, in no hurry to disperse.
I muse on the privilege of living in Jerusalem; the interaction with special people that we have. And the contagious joy from these so-called 'hopeless' cases that I take home with me.

IF YOU DON'T BELIEVE IN MIRACLES...
YOU ARE NOT A REALIST!!!

12

'Simple Miracles'

The year 2003 began with Gulf War II looming and like the last time, Israel had to prepare itself for any eventuality. In February, we received new gasmasks for the whole family, with a special one for small children. The plastic hood had a rubber hose attached to a battery-operated motor. When we tried it on, Na'il looked like an astronaut. He became so obsessed with the mask that we had to hide it, and let him play with the box instead.

Throughout the country, heavy winter rains turned little streams into roaring rivers, and daily, the news mentioned how many centimeters the Sea of Galilee had risen! That surely was good news, which wasn't in big supply those days.
 And then it began to snow. Again! We never expected to see so much snow in Israel. Sunday, February 23, a snow alert was given for Jerusalem. Monday, around noon, the first flakes began to fall. By 2 p.m. all schools had shut their doors and concerned residents rushed home, causing major traffic jams.

On Friday, the children were still at home, enjoying the unexpected holiday. Na'il kept bringing his yellow boots to us, so Wim and I took turns 'trudging' through the heavy snow with him. This child would have loved to stay out all day. On the balcony near the living room, Wim built a snowman which he dubbed "Benny White II".

Because Na'il sometimes suffered from 'tics', we were referred to Hadassah hospital for an E.E.G. Excited to go to hospital, he was surprised to see Mahmud, who had to sign for the sedation. Because Na'il was going to miss out most of the 'real fun' by being sedated, I took lots of pictures for him to enjoy afterwards. The test results were normal, and they never found the reason for the tics. Later I began to see a pattern - Na'il only had 'tics' when he wasn't feeling 100%; they were gone when he was his old self again.

The staff of the Ma'ayan school wanted me to teach them basic sign language. It was so much fun, and I always loved it when more people became enthusiastic about this wonderful expressive communication tool. Due to his contractured arms and fingers, Na'il couldn't sign back but he did understand the basic signs.

Because of the looming war, no one was in the mood to celebrate Purim. Our 'sealed room' (built-in bomb shelter) was stocked up with canned vegetables and bottled water.
Even the weather fit the country's mood: dust-filled skies preceded thunderstorms. Our lives were interwoven with threats of war and the everyday cares of a special needs family. We believed that each day held the possibility of miracles.

It was even better than a party! To rule out albinism related eye problems the eye specialist wanted to take special eye photos. Na'il ignored his mother Sameera and little sister when they arrived in Hadassah hospital to sign the consent form for the sedation.
    "Let's try sedation via a suppository first," the anesthetist suggested.
It had the opposite effect on Na'il. Instead of becoming relaxed, he almost jumped out of the children's cot. Neither did he become sleepy, but more and more enthusiastic and hyperactive.
    "This sometimes happens with these children," the doctor told me. "Unfortunately, because of the suppository, I can't give him an additional intravenous sedative."

We had no choice but to undergo the eye test while Na'il was wide awake. It was quite a struggle to keep him still, for everything was sooooooo exciting!

I had read about Cochlear implants, an electronic device that allowed deaf children to hear and felt that such a device would benefit Na'il and help his development.
It wasn't difficult to get Dr. Sheffer, our genetics doctor enthusiastic - she immediately wrote two referrals.

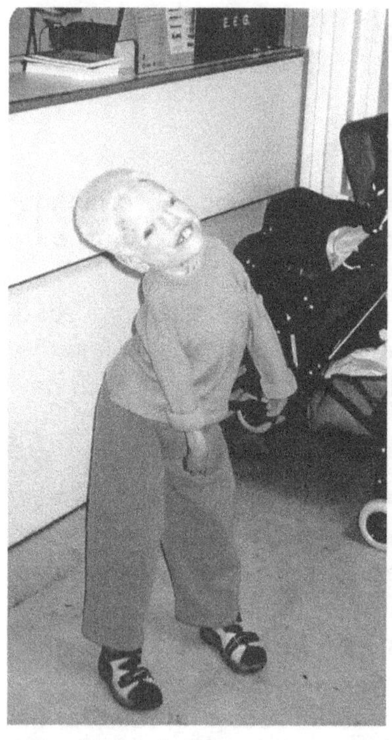

It was a happy month for Na'il. The CT scan of his ear canals was done in another hospital. After signing the consent form, Mahmud stayed with his son for a little while. This time, Na'il was sedated properly and slept during the procedure. It struck me that Mahmud really loved his son. Na'il however was standoffish, and more interested in his IV.

By the end of March, more snow, hail and storms blew over the country. A few days later, the winter weather changed into a heat wave! This, together with the garbage strike made Jerusalem stink! How true was the saying, "In Israel, life doesn't go by you ~ it goes through you!"

We couldn't have given Na'il a better present - he had to start orthodontic treatment. From Nadia's orthodontic treatment, we knew Professor Becker was an expert in dealing with very difficult orthodontic cases. Many people called him a "mensch". Na'il's first phase was a simple brace. He liked the fitting and fiddling; however, wearing the device wasn't his piece of cake.

"Well…." Professor Becker grinned. "He's a challenge, but we're going to win!"

Na'il became the star of the show on the second-floor orthodontic department. Our little guy always brought laughter and hilarity the moment he walked in.

Na'il turned nine on May 27. He was growing taller, but not fatter, and I remembered the Alyn doctor who once told me with a twinkle in his eyes, "Stop thinking like a Yiddische mama! He will never grow fat!"

The school party was celebrated in a shaded area outside the classroom. As always it was full of games, songs, laughter and presents. We felt so privileged to be part of this special group of people!

Na'il had 'outgrown' Joke, the Dutch volunteer who had taken him on so many outings. His needs didn't match her possibilities any more, and now it was Wim's turn to take Na'il for long walks to parks and playgrounds. He seemed to have a nose for them. With his leg, he would point in the direction Wim had to take him. Many times, rounding a corner in a previously unknown area, to Wim's amazement they stumbled upon another small playground – a new area to explore. Sometimes children screamed and ran away. Thankfully there were others, mostly the religious children, who asked questions and accepted Na'il for who he was. Because special needs children were an integrated part of their neighborhoods, they were used to interacting with them.

> *"Living in Israel is to live in a place*
> *where very little gets taken for granted,*
> *where even the simplest things*
> *are often seen for the miracles they are."*

For us, meeting open minded children and adults fell in that category. Added to that was another, even bigger miracle - war was averted. For now.

The summer holiday loomed - two whole weeks of having to rack our brains on how to keep Na'il from being bored to death. This, combined with very hot weather, was not exactly my favorite time of the year. Wim took time off from work, and Na'il accompanied his father on his rounds through the city. Of course, part of Na'il's holiday activities consisted of extra time in the bathtub.

Keftsuba was a small Luna park not far from Jerusalem, a favorite place for school trips. Na'il loved it, especially the bumper cars. I wasn't too happy about those, and kept a watchful eye on father and son who had the time of their lives. I was exhausted by the time we went home but at least we had given Na'il an outing he loved.

A few days later we took Na'il and Nadia to a huge Luna park near the coast. The children loved it, and to my amazement, I began to enjoy myself as well. Being so close to the Mediterranean Sea, the breeze made the high temperatures bearable.

Na'il's favorites were the cable car and the Ferris wheel. In the days that followed, Na'il constantly dragged his photo album to us. Then, smiling his glorious, sweet and hopeful smile, he would point to the Ferris wheel. Or the bumper cars, or....

In November, Wim went to Holland for a long overdue visit to family and friends, while I 'guarded the fort' and took care of the children and the animals.

"I'll stay with Na'il," our neighbor Zehava offered. "You take the dogs for a walk."

When I returned after ten minutes, Zehava ran up to me. "You won't believe it!"

As Na'il had seen me leave, I wondered what he had been up to.

"The moment you were out the door," Zehava laughed, "Na'il immediately went to the TV/video, stuck his foot in the recorder, turned on the TV, played with the light switches and then rushed to the bathroom to turn on the tap...."

In record time, he had managed to do everything he knew was forbidden. *So much for asking Zehava to keep an eye on him,* I thought.

"I tried to look stern," Zehava said, "and waved my finger in front of him, but he just laughed in my face and continued with his 'rampage'."

The next time I had to walk the dogs I made sure Na'il didn't see me leave.

Two days before Wim was scheduled to return to Israel, Nadia began to behave aggressively towards Fahima. Her behavior deteriorated even more, but I thought this was just another 'problem' we had to deal with and left it for what it was. (We had been through so many crises with Moshiko, who suffered from Borderline Personality Disorder, that I figured we'd survive this too!)
However, Nadia's deaf school told me to see a psychiatrist, and after a long, exhausting day, Nadia was diagnosed with a psychosis and admitted to the psychiatric ward on Mount Scopus hospital, on the other side of town.

It was the beginning of a very intense, traumatic and exhausting period. In order to care for Nadia's physical needs (for which the nurses didn't have time) I visited her twice, sometimes three times a day. At the same time, preparations were under way for Na'il's Cochlear Implant. I took him to Hadassah Ein Kerem for an MRI of his head. A few days later, we visited the audiology department for another hearing test. Na'il thought it was wonderful and exciting!

The day he began to vomit, had diarrhea and a high fever, as usual we ended up in Hadassah's emergency department. Our little boy was more than happy when the doctors hooked him up to an IV and kept him overnight. Only the next afternoon did they release the dehydrated little boy, and were we allowed to go home again. Our lives felt like a roller coaster ride.
Too weak to return to school, Na'il didn't mind I took him along to help Nadia, who was still hospitalized on Mount Scopus. Wim always took him when he visited Nadia in the afternoons. Of course, the little boy loved the unexplored territory - this was a completely new hospital for him.

It was the end of December 2003, and we looked back to a very eventful year. It wasn't easy to take our problems one at a time when they refused to get in line. But somehow, by the grace of God, we had survived.

With renewed hope, we looked forward to what 2004 was going to bring us.

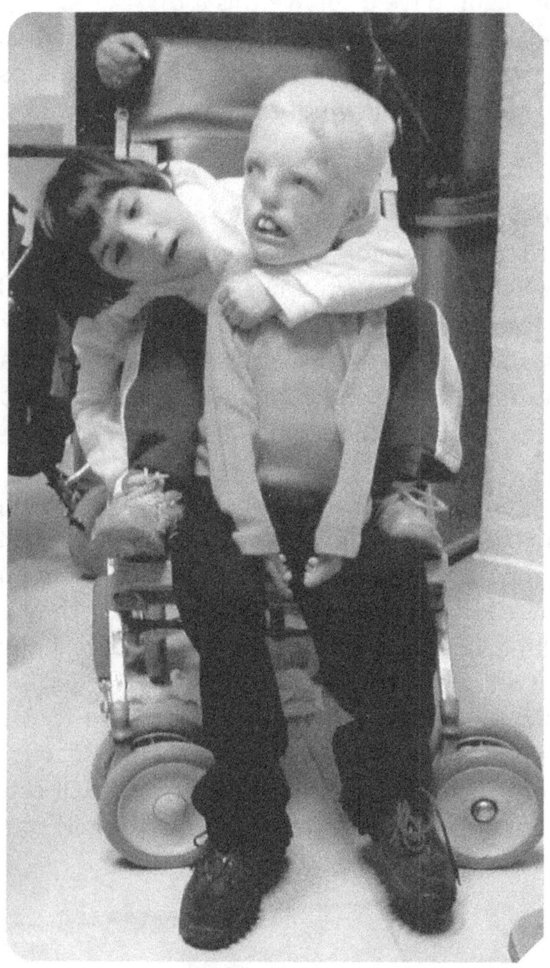

Na'il isn't so sure he likes his overly affectionate friend

13

Hurts and Trials and Times of Growth

"In this life we will encounter hurts and trial that we will not be able to change - we are just going to have to let them change us."
Ron Lee Davis

The year 2004 began with big question marks: should we go ahead with Na'il's scheduled Cochlear implant? Would Nadia's emotional and mental health be strong enough to cope with my absence when I stayed with Na'il during the hospitalization? How would she handle the shift in attention- from her to Na'il when she was finally released after two months in hospital?

In February, Israel experienced an earthquake. It wasn't a 'big' one, only 5 on the Richter scale, with the epicenter near the Dead Sea. I felt it, and many people saw high-rise buildings sway – a frightening experience. Three days later, more excitement - a snow storm closed Jerusalem again. "Out-of-towners" flocking to the capital, created even more havoc on the roads.
There was also excitement closer to home: as a preventive measure before the operation Na'il needed a meningitis immunization. While I took pictures, our neighbor the doctor administered the shot. Na'il was fascinated with the pictures. Tapping with his toe on the one with the syringe was his way of asking for more…. He was a special child indeed!

February 22 began with our car refusing to start, which made me miss the Brit Milah (circumcision) of a friend's first born son. Another bus was blown to pieces by a brainwashed Arab terrorist, killing school children, parents and a soldier. More than sixty people were wounded. It was the 110th suicide bombing in the last 3½ years of violence. Would it ever stop?

A technician who was supposed to come to the house to hook us up to the ADSL, (fast internet) called off at the last minute. Wim drove to Ben Gurion airport to pick up his American 'Mom', Betsy. He left his coat (with the keys) in the car, closed the trunk and locked himself out. A special (expensive) service unlocked the car by using a metal coat hanger. At least Wim and Betsy made it safely back to Jerusalem!

Both Nadia and Fahima came down with the flu – complete with running noses and nasty coughs. *What if Na'il becomes sick too?* I wondered. When it looked as if Fahima was developing pneumonia, I really became worried. *I won't be able to handle two hospitalizations at the same time Lord! We need a big miracle!* I prayed.

Thankfully, everything turned out fine.

Na'il's pre-operative blood tests were done at his health clinic, a place he had never been before. I usually went there to fight for the necessary permits. His pediatrician came out of her office to meet her patient for the first time.

"Beside his syndrome, Na'il is a healthy boy!" I always joked.

That year, Purim was celebrated with the usual fervor and Na'il loved his pirate costume, which came with a 'hook'. Together with Dutch friends we celebrated Fahima's and Nadia's birthday. All the guests were 'dressed up' for Purim, which Na'il loved. At one point, he became curious what the adults were drinking. He never drank anything but his milk formula, and always refused to taste something else. To our amazement Na'il took a sip of the wine. He liked it and went from friend to friend, begging for a sip, laughing all the time. It was such a ball, especially when he tried to blow out the candles before its time, and it wasn't even his birthday yet!

Tuesday, March 9. Time to start packing our hospital bags.

Mahmud had to come to the hospital to sign for the operation and I asked him if he needed to be reminded.

"I'll be there," he said. "No need to call me the day before."

When Na'il saw the picture book I had made in preparation for his operation, he got so excited! We had taped a BBC program about a cochlear implant and tried to watch it together with Na'il, but he preferred to watch his dentist video instead. I had filmed his dental treatment which included many close-ups, and he never tired of watching it. Wednesday, March 10, 8.30 a.m. Hadassah Hospital

E.N.T. (Ear Nose Throat) clinic.

"We can't register Na'il without the biological father present. He has to sign the papers," the nurse informed me. "And he better hurry, for you have a busy schedule before the operation."

I fumbled for my cell phone and called Mahmud. "Where are you?"

"Oops! I forgot! I'm on my way!"

My heart sank. *Will all my planning be in vain because of this stupid mishap?* I thought.

Even though Mahmud showed up half an hour later, the 'list' was already messed up. On the children's ward, a nurse asked me all kind of questions. "Which number wife are you?"

I didn't understand what she meant, until it dawned upon me that she presumed Mahmud and I were married. We had a good laugh about it. When we had to see the next person on the 'list', I was prepared,

"I'm Na'il's foster Mom."

The anesthesia nurse made Na'il's day by giving him an oxygen mask to take home!

We had to wait a very long time before the doctor had time to see Na'il. Then the new computer program refused to cooperate. Na'il didn't mind, if I allowed him to 'drool' over all kinds of (fearsome looking) medical tools. Plain 'waiting' was another story. When the computer finally cooperated, the doctor explained the operation to Mahmud, who then signed the papers. I could see he was more than happy to return to work and leave me to deal with the rest of his son's upcoming operation.

Na'il and I were ushered into a room full of doctors in white and green coats.

"This is Na'il, a patient with Klein-Waardenburg Syndrome," one of the doctors began his talk.

Scanning the room, Na'il singled out a doctor in green and walked up to him. The doctor in charge continued to explain the surgical procedure and give personal background information on Na'il. However, most of his colleagues only had eyes and ears for Na'il. Uncertain, and a bit embarrassed, the doctor in green looked at me.

"What does he want?"

"He wants to sit on your lap."

Over and over, the doctor tried to explain "patient Na'il" to his audience, but nobody listened – everyone was in stitches about Na'il's behavior. We made such a ruckus that Professor Elidan stuck his head around the door to see what all that noise was about.

It was always like this - Na'il's doctor's visits always caused laughter and merriment, because he just LOVED them. Of course, a very unusual phenomenon!

At the end of an exhausting day, the nurse from the surgical children's ward gave us permission to go home for the night. I was ready to crash! It had been a SUPER day for Na'il.

Thursday, March 11. A splitting headache didn't bode well for the long and heavy day ahead of us - I was going to need every ounce of energy and strength I had. Prayer, strong medication and Coca Cola kept me going.

Back on children's surgery, Na'il became the 'star-of-the-ward'. The delayed operation gave him lots of time to explore the many interesting rooms of his favorite ward.

Finally, an auxiliary nurse took us to the operation suites. 'Dressed up' as usual I accompanied Na'il to a side room. From his hospital bed, he got a glimpse of the operating theatre and it made him so excited that he almost jumped out of his bed! Everyone laughed their heads off, and the highlight was when I put him onto the operating table. He deeply inhaled the first anesthesia and was instantly asleep.

"Bye, bye, Ima!" the anesthetist said.

I had to leave. One last kiss, a glance over my shoulder and I had to leave my precious little one in the hands of qualified medical staff and Na'il's guarding angels.

Neither the CT scan nor the MRI had shown anatomical differences of Na'il's inner ear. However, after the three-hour operation professor Elidan told me there had been some surprises. "But it looks like everything will be all right," he put me at ease.

Around 8 p.m. Na'il returned to the children's ward. We now were in intermediate care - a big room with seven other patients and their mothers.

Except for the expected headache Na'il did very well and loved every minute of his hospitalization - even the blood tests.

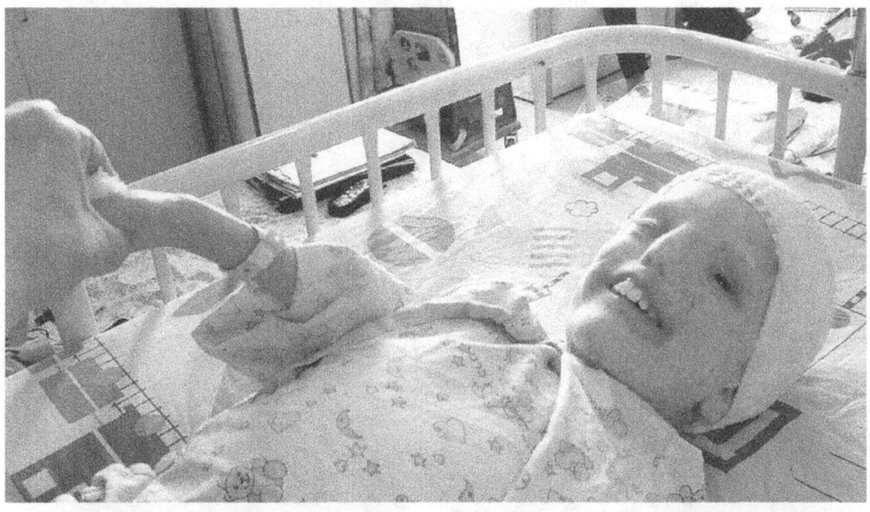

A visit from his biological family created confusion amongst the mainly Arab mothers with whom I shared the room. Because they spoke Arabic with Na'il's parents, I didn't understand why Sameera suddenly burst into tears.

"What's the matter?" I asked Mahmud in Hebrew.

"These women think you are Na'il's real mother, because you love him so much," he explained.

I was embarrassed and felt sorry for Sameera.

March 15 Na'il was released from hospital but had to stay home till the staples (yes, really) were removed. Because of our spacious house and easy entrance Na'il's class and teachers could pay him a visit. He enjoyed the attention, and the children were blessed with an unexpected outing.

Na'il loved to look at the many pictures I took during the hospitalization. With his foot, he kept tapping on the one with the suitcases standing by the stairs and the operating theatre – he wanted to go back to the hospital! Funny guy!

The wound needed time to heal, and the swollen tissue to get back to normal. On April 25, we were scheduled to fit Na'il's sound processor. This time, we were the excited ones! We had waited so long for this moment! Na'il was cranky because he had to wait a long time in the boring, empty corridor. Another boy was fitted with a shetel, and we heard his screams through the door. How is Na'il going to react, I wondered?

The small room was packed with the teacher, aide, speech therapist, music teacher, three audiologists and the three of us! While I tried to keep Na'il occupied with a thick picture booklet, Wim filmed the whole process. Finally, after time consuming computer measurements, the processor was switched on. Of course, we had been speculating how Na'il's reaction would be. Would he respond with a "gggchchchc!" meaning happy, or an "Ah, ah, ah" noise, or "Oh, oh, oh!" sound?

As always, Na'il surprised everyone.
When the first sound was transmitted, Na'il sat absolutely still with a look of total surprise on his face. Gradually, this turned into the sweetest and most beautiful smile we had ever seen from him. Almost everyone in the room had tears in their eyes.

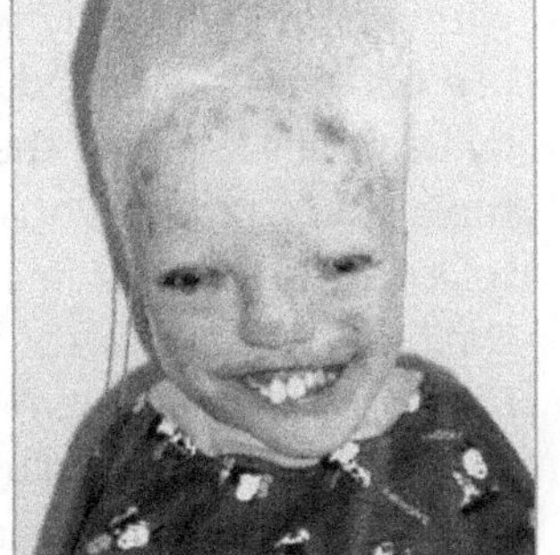

   "Na'il's hearing development is like that of a baby," the audiology staff informed us.

   "Because his brain has to learn to distinguish between sounds, the program has to be build up, stage by stage." Each additional sound level that was fed into the processor brought the same, sweet, extra special smile on his face.

Na'il was already past the age for learning to speak, but together with the communication board, and the *shetel,* as it was called in Hebrew, we were in for exciting times. Busy and intensive too, but we gladly invested our time and energy to give this precious little boy more opportunities to grow and develop.

Each morning when we 'hooked' Na'il up to the device, he treated us with the same, glorious, sweet smile only he could give!

It seemed our lives revolved around hospitals. Na'il didn't mind if it was his own hospitalization (although he preferred that), or someone else's. Nadia's bladder infection turned kidney infection, turned hospitalization. Welcome to floor 5, room 5, of Hadassah hospital. We re-entered this special world called hospital life. Being cooped up in a room with four other patients often created 'instant' families. The patient in the best condition helped the helpless ones. Family members, visiting their loved ones on a regular basis, brought their own lively stories.

Nadia needed around the clock care, which meant I stayed with her from 7 a.m. till 7 p.m. Wim took over the evening and night shift, and tried to sleep in an 'easy' chair next to Nadia's bed.

Of course, Na'il LOVED to visit his big sister, and roam the (for him) new ward. It had many 'exciting' things, like catheter bags and other medical appliances. He was disappointed when Nadia was discharged and the daily hospital visits ended.

Na'il was excited to sit in the chair of the orthodontist and be fitted with a brace. Actually wearing it was another matter. Being unable to use his arms, he found other ways to remove the dental brace: either by using his knee, or the corner of a table or cupboard. It made us and the school staff nervous, for we were afraid that one day, he was going to lose the expensive thing. Neither punishment nor threats helped, Na'il saw it as a sport.

Professor Becker laughed when I told him about Na'il's clever antics.

"I think I have a solution." He drilled a few holes in the plastic. "He was able to create a vacuum with his tongue," he explained. "Now he can't do that anymore."

With a "Good luck!" we were sent on our way. Five minutes later, Na'il managed to send the brace flying again! I went back to the Professor. The dear man laughed and shook his head in disbelief.

"I hate to admit it," he said, "but it seems this little guy has won! Let's wait another year. Perhaps he will be more cooperative then."

I really hoped so, but wasn't sure about that!

It was a long, hot summer, and then Nadia got the flu. Or so we thought. It turned out to be a sepsis (blood poisoning) caused by her kidney problems. The only way to solve the recurrent infections was by inserting a catheter directly into the kidney. Na'il didn't leave her side when she finally came home with two catheter bags attached to her walker!

Nadia's room now resembled a private clinic. I often found Na'il 'drooling' over the medical supply tray, eying the syringes that he loved to 'steal' and hide in his room.

"You know you are fatigued when you sit at a stop sign, waiting for it to turn green," I read in one of Barbara Johnson's books. How I needed a fresh dose of humor to keep going!

The hectic days blended into weeks and months, and by now it was November. Nadia was hospitalized again for the removal of a stent. The day of the operation coincided with a seminar about Cochlear implants for special needs children, in which Na'il was the showcase. Around noon, when Nadia was stable enough, I raced down to the auditorium and was just in time to hear the part about Na'il. Seeing that first 'hook-up' again on the auditorium's big screen, brought new tears to my eyes - it was so special!

What was supposed to be a 'simple' stent removal procedure, turned into another blood-poisoning, which took Nadia nine days to recover. The moment Na'il returned from school he 'demanded' to go to hospital to visit Nadia. After an impatient wait, Wim usually took him there around 5 p.m. The first thing Na'il always did on the ward was to check the doctor's room. Why it was his most favorite place we never understood, for we didn't find anything special in there.

An Arab doctor took a liking to Na'il. When he was on duty, he'd take him in his arms to the male patients, telling them about the special boy. Being with people who accepted him for who he was, Na'il didn't suffer from shyness - he loved every minute of it!

When one of the male Arab nurses heard Na'il 'collected' syringes (without the needle), he began to give him a different one each time he saw him. Na'il continued to bring laughter and joy, just by being himself.

During those strenuous times, I desperately needed a 'handle' to keep going while trying to focus on God's grace and strength.

"When we choose to say: I'm exactly where I'm supposed to be at this moment in time, we stop wasting precious time and emotional energy wishing things were different, or wanting another set of circumstances." Charles Swindoll's wise words were a comfort during those times of hardship. Through it all, we learned not only to be content, but truly thankful.

Despite all the hardships, there were so many blessings: the special people we got to know while being in hospital; the lady from the coffee shop, who, after she heard about our special needs family, always gave me a discount; the security guards, who let us through without checking our bags, because they knew us by now.

And then it was again *Chanukah*, the Festival of Light, one of Na'il's favorite holidays. Not because of the *sufganiots* or the latkes, or the dreidels, but because there were always so many candles he could blow out....

It had been another intense year. But again, God had been our strong Tower, an ever-present help in trouble.

14

More Learning Experiences

In January 2005, we found ourselves again on Ward 5, room 5, for what we hoped would be Nadia's last urological operation.

That Sunday morning, Na'il had neither seen me pack nor leave. When he came home from school and didn't find me, (probably also noticed a wheelchair was missing), he went straight to Nadia's room. Finding the room empty, he immediately pulled his buggy from under the stair case. Then he took Wim to the cupboard in which I had hidden his red 'hospital' bag. Smiling, and 'pointing' with his head, he 'asked' Wim to take it out.   Our very perceptive little boy was ready to go to hospital too. He knew! Much to his chagrin, Wim didn't take him straight away. Eventually he accepted his father's promise that they would go there, later.

Spring in Israel is always a glorious time. Thanks to the blessed winter rains, everything was painted an abundant green and yellow. Martin Buber voiced it like this:

"The God of history and the God of nature cannot be separated, and the land of Israel is a token of their unity."

I always preferred to take the dogs for a walk through the uncultivated areas of our neighborhood. This way, I could feast my eyes on the beauty around me: the Jerusalem spurge cascading from the rocks, creating a flowery carpet; the ever-present Cape Sorrel, which looks like clover and even invaded the pot plants on our balcony. Then the mimosa seedlings (Acacia) blooming their fluffy heart out on every available spot; yellow broom lined the roadsides and could be seen between the rocks.

Next to yellow was that unique color green - bright, soft and fresh, which only could be seen in early spring. When the sun caressed the damp earth after a spring shower, the new grass sprouted up and willed the trees to burst their buds.

Our Bedouin girls, born with a rare genetic syndrome, participated in a genetic research project. A doctor from Be'er Sheva came to our house to get some DNA blood samples and was still there when Na'il returned from school. Immediately, he rushed over to the yellow/red bucket in which needles were discarded. In hospital, Na'il always peeked inside those buckets, and knew exactly what they were used for. He was very upset when I told him he couldn't play with it.

One balmy April afternoon, while enjoying the view from our balcony, I mused about opening lines for our upcoming newsletter:
"The swallows still high up in the air, screeching while joyfully hunting for insects; the traffic slowly picking up after the Shabbat's rest… And we don't know what awaits us in the week to come…." Where on earth did that thought come from? I wondered. I was soon to find out.

Sunday morning, Na'il woke up with a fever and really looked sick, so I kept him home. Usually, even with the flu, he was still active and alert. This time however, he was apathetic and groaning softly. Something wasn't right and when he stopped drinking, we took him to Hadassah's Emergency Department. When he didn't seem to realize where he was I knew he was really ill. In the previous months, several Israeli children had died from meningitis. In order to rule out the infectious disease, the doctor ordered a battery of tests.
Only when the spinal tap came out clear, did they transfer Na'il to the third-floor children's ward. Finally, I could lie down on a (real) foldable bed. Nothing spectacular showed up in the blood tests, but to be on the safe side, the doctor started Na'il on intravenous antibiotics. This must have done the trick, for on the third day Na'il became more interested in his surroundings. He still didn't realize he was in his beloved hospital.
Still weak, but feeling much better, it was on the fourth day that our little boy began to explore the ward on his scooter. When he saw a poster bearing the "Hadassah" logo, he kept tapping it with his feet. I tried to explain he already was there, but he didn't grasp it. On the last day of the hospitalization we had to exit the building and return again. Only then the penny dropped. And then it was time to go home!

Pesach is the holiday when most Israelis kept *"Kosher le Pesach"* and only ate matzot, unleavened bread for a whole week. This year we held a small Seder meal, together with our family and closest friends. This Biblical holiday is a real family holiday. Many people travel throughout the country, clogging up the roads, and filling parks and attractions to overflowing. We had learned our lesson, and except for a short trip to the mall, we stayed home and relaxed. Throughout the years, our children's needs had changed quite dramatically. We also didn't have enough hands to manage all the wheelchairs and buggy, which didn't fit into one car anyhow.

Na'il and his *Abba* were the only ones who went out, always in search for new playgrounds. Our little boy continued to try out new places. First, he carefully looked things over, to see what it held in store for him. It could happen that the playground wasn't to his liking after all. Then he motioned Wim to continue – in search of the next one. At one stage, swings were his favorite. Not far from our house was a small playground with a 'safe' swing, in which he could sit by himself. Wim pushed him, higher and higher, over a hundred times, and he still loved it. Feeling free, zooming through the air, he smiled, beamed and sometimes squealed with laughter. Then he was as happy as could be! Our precious little boy! Swings continued to be his favorite play things until his back began to give him too many problems.

Stress could be of your own making; it could also be caused by pride. Afterwards, I scolded myself for being stupid enough to think that I could do it all. But by then it was too late and it seemed that everything was falling apart.

Even though Moshiko didn't live with us any more, we had promised to guide him through an elbow operation in Hadassah hospital, scheduled for May 22nd. Two weeks later, Na'il was scheduled to undergo a tendon release operation. I barely survived the emotional onslaught of Moshiko's behavior, but I had to go on and prepare for the next steeplechase.

"I've never seen a child like this before," the spine specialist said. Because of the worsening scoliosis, Na'il had to be fitted with a "Boston Brace", (corset) to keep his spine from becoming even more crooked. A few days before his operation, I took him to the orthopedic workshop. Na'il was excited to be 'plastered' in and loved it when I put him in the sink to wash it off again. The end product looked (and must have felt) like a straight-jacket. He wasn't cooperative when we put it on, but in the end understood he had to wear it every day.

The moment he returned home I took it off immediately, wondering why we had to torment the little guy so much. This scoliosis needs an operation, not a brace! According to the specialist, Na'il was too young for such a major operation. He just had to learn to live with that despised Boston Brace….

June 5. It was Na'il's turn to be hospitalized. Of course, he loved every minute of it. I always used visual tools to explain things to Na'il. This time, I made him another special photo album, explaining all the stages he would have to go through. It became his constant companion and he kept himself busy for hours on end, drooling over pictures of surgeons, nurses holding up big needles, and operating rooms. In the evening, we finally installed ourselves in the small, two-bed room on the children's surgical ward.

"Can we go home now?" I asked the nurse on duty.

"Home? Of course not! You'll have to stay overnight!" she replied. That was something I hadn't counted on. Nothing could be done to persuade the nurse. "Sorry, but those are the rules."

Na'il didn't mind – he loved his big hospital bed!

Early the next morning, the staff in the operating room welcomed me warmly and laughed about Na'il's enthusiasm. When he saw the oxygen mask, he squealed from joy. The anesthetist roared with laughter when he deeply inhaled the first anesthesia.

"Oh, you're a narcoman (addict)" she exclaimed.

Like Professor Elidan had when he operated on Na'il, Dr. Joseph too encountered anatomical surprises. He had a hard time removing little pieces of bone which had grown between the hip tendons.

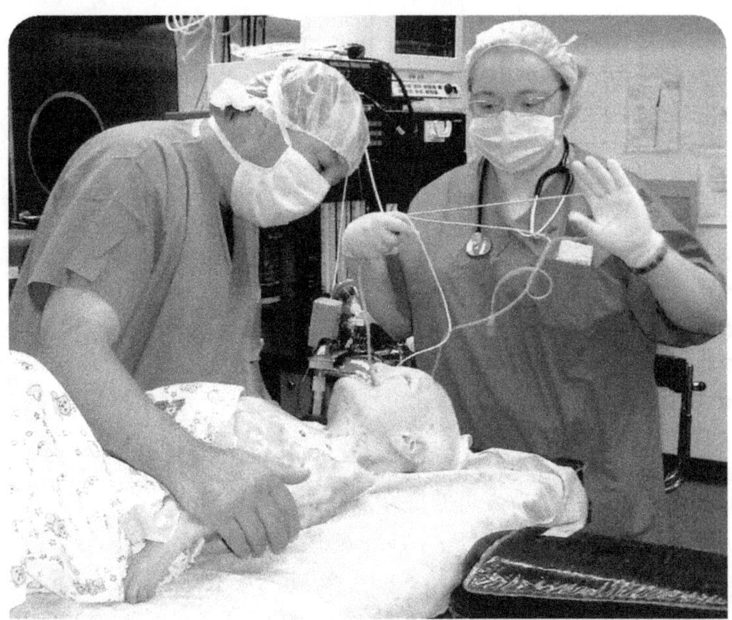

A big smile on the operating table

To prevent them from growing back again, Na'il underwent a radiation session a few hours after the surgery.
It was late by the time we returned to intermediate care on the children's ward. I longed to lie down but then Na'il's family showed up. Inwardly I groaned. Despite the splitting headache, I smiled and told them about their son's operation.

We knew that the hospitalization in Hadassah would be a short one. Na'il was to receive further treatment in Alyn hospital and we were transferred by a Hadassah ambulance. Knowing the Israeli driving habits, I was afraid Na'il would fall, so I sat on the floor next to him, holding onto his buggy for dear life.
Na'il wasn't a child that could be left alone. Because he needed 24-hour care, Wim took over the usual night duty, while I stayed with him during the days. It was almost Shavuot and I was grateful there were no other patients to share Na'il's room. The only thing I wanted was to have some peace and quiet.

I had expected them to start with physiotherapy right away, but nothing happened during the holidays. When I asked the head nurse, it turned out they had forgotten us!

"Can't we take him home for the weekend?" I pleaded.

"Sorry, you can't," the nurse informed me. "Doctor doesn't allow a child to leave when he still has stitches."

We had no other alternative than to grit our teeth and keep going. It was hard, because Na'il was bored to death. The only thing he wanted was to get out of his room and be on the move. Because the wound was still too fresh and tender he couldn't use his scooter. This meant WE constantly had to take him for a walk.

Barbara Johnson described the weeks that followed perfectly:

"During this stage, we didn't have a lot of choices about how to spend our time. We simply stumbled along, from one crisis to the next. Our lives seemed to be controlled by whatever blow hit us next, sending us lurching from headache to headache, to horror story. We chose to hold on to the ONE Who promises never to leave us, no matter how insane the circumstances got."

Na'il was in and out of Alyn hospital - first as an out-patient, and then hospitalized again. Koos, the Dutch physiotherapist who had known

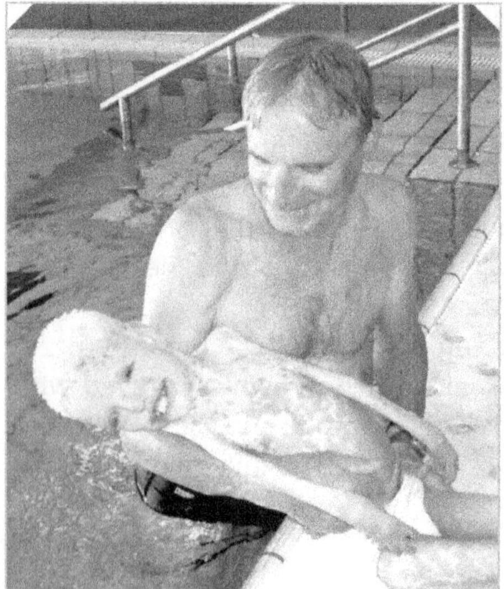

Na'il since he was a toddler, worked with him. Because he was still in great pain, Na'il didn't cooperate very much. Even the work-outs in the pool with Abe, the man who knew Na'il since his first days in Alyn and taught him to 'swim', didn't do the trick.

Refusing to stand on his left leg, he hopped in the water like a stork.

In the end, they let Na'il do his own thing, which was such a relief for me. My heart ached for the little boy, who suffered much pain after that horrible and traumatic operation. He needed to do things on his own pace, in his own time.

The only 'good' thing that came out of this difficult hospitalization was that Na'il's food changed. We hoped the "Nutren" formula would help our 13-kilo boy gain some weight. He continued to drink from his (baby) bottle, but we were told that this higher calorie formula would give him his much-needed energy. It would also help him to build up his strength after the operation.

Looking back on the year that was, we realized there had been many crises. Somewhere I read that the Chinese sign for crisis was like the one for opportunity. A crisis could be a disaster, or an opportunity for growth. What a wise way to put it! I knew we had grown that year. It was a miracle we were still able to smile, and find the humor in situations. We didn't have a choice – we either smiled or cried!

Na'il often brought a smile on our faces, just by being himself. His sweet, naughty, precious, curious little self. We thanked God for giving us this extra special child to love and care for!

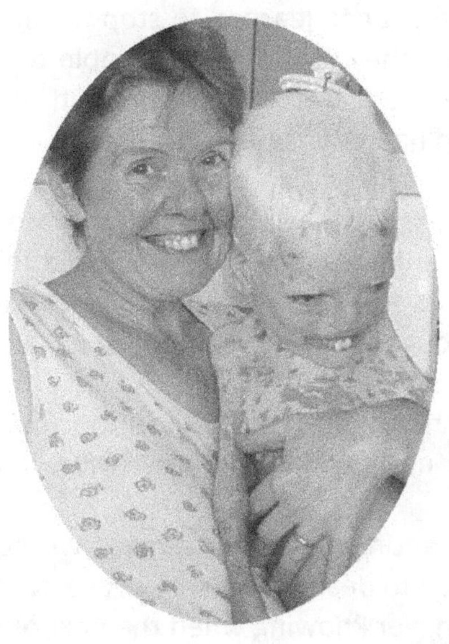

15

"Life is not measured with the quantity of breaths you take, but with the quantity of moments that took your breath away."

The year 2006 contained many situations that took our breath away – both in a positive and negative way. In connection to Na'il's wheelchair application, there were hold-ups, surprises, more paper work, and finally the promise that a special committee would consider the matter and decide.

Our crazy, hectic life often left us breathless. We had to deal with Israel's red-tape on a regular basis, lived a 24/7/365 life with multiple-needs children and added to that, the constant strain of financial worries. These daily challenges caused a unique kind of stress. In order to survive the marathon that seemed to be our lives, we had to find ways to deal with it.

"You should do this...."

"You shouldn't do that...."

The outsiders meant well, but their advice didn't help much. Throughout the years, I had learned to stop feeling guilty, or trying to explain it to people - they would never be able to understand or have an inkling how we lived. Backseat drivers and armchair critics were part of our lives and had to be endured.

Thank God for books. We had plenty to choose from to help and encourage us. One subtitle read, "... a book of tools that can turn life into a gift to be enjoyed, rather than a sentence to be served." Now that was a great thought to ponder about for a while!

Moshiko's psychiatric problems became too much for me to handle. After an especially nasty incident my eyes finally opened and I said:

"Enough!"

Na'il was such a comfort during those heart wrenching times. Unable to talk, we never had to deal with verbal abuse. Neither did we have to walk on eggshells, never knowing when the next outburst would occur.

Our little boy didn't twist my words and turn me into a liar. Na'il didn't manipulate and try to sow discord on every possible occasion, nor did he laugh when I was ready to burst into tears. Na'il, our little sunshine, never woke up cranky or in a bad mood; he was a willing and cooperative child - a wonderful, sweet, naughty and curious boy who never complained when things didn't go according to plan. He never cried or whined when he had to solve a problem. He faced it and then set out to tackle it- he just did it! Na'il's outlook on life was exactly how Hudson Taylor described the way God worked:

"There are three stages in the work of God:
Impossible - Difficult - Done."

To me, Na'il had been God's gift, a sweet comfort to hold, cuddle and shower with kisses. He gave so much back by just being himself. He took my breath away. We communicated on an emotional level that was unique. It was as if he intuitively knew what was going on. I'm a Highly Sensitive Person (HSP), perhaps that's why he was extra special to me. But even though I loved him to pieces, I was always very strict with him. But that's what he needed, and he felt safe within the boundaries we set for him.

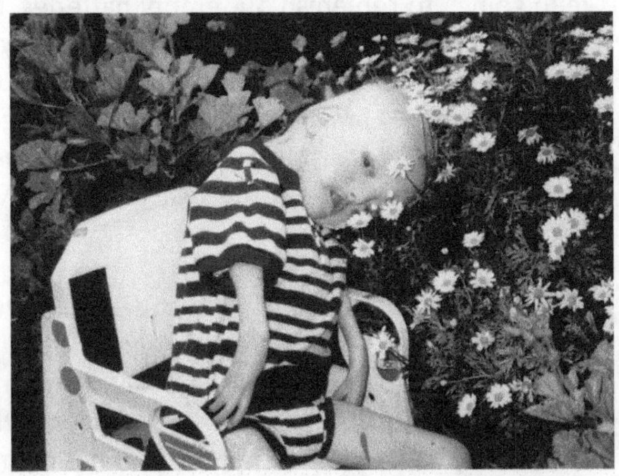

We were grateful that he accepted both Wim and me completely - as long as one of us was at home, he was all right.

New people in his life were always a challenge for him. For us too, as we were never sure if he was going to accept them or not. New volunteers always had to learn how Na'il 'ticked', which meant that either Wim or I (usually me) had to accompany the volunteer during those first times. I always dreaded those trial visits and often lacked the energy.

Itamar was a new volunteer, willing to take Na'il once a week for a two -hour walk. Wim showed him Na'il's favorite spots and warned him,

"It's of utmost importance that Na'il knows who the boss is!"

I wasn't sure if it would work out with this nice young man, but he was young and energetic, so we decided to give it a try. Na'il was happy as long as he was 'on the go'. We were grateful it worked out well with Itamar.

Taking care of the children was a ministry with mostly output and hardly any input. Burn-out always lurked in the shadows.

"When having to deal with chronic stress, diversions can be a gift to give ourselves," I read somewhere. For Wim, this meant reading devotional or biographical books. I, on the other hand, needed to 'escape' into a novel or romantic movie. Each of us had to find our own way to 'keep going', to replenish our empty batteries, to continue the job the Lord had given us to do. Being each other's 'yoke-fellow' was such a blessing, for this was a 'job' you couldn't do on your own. I

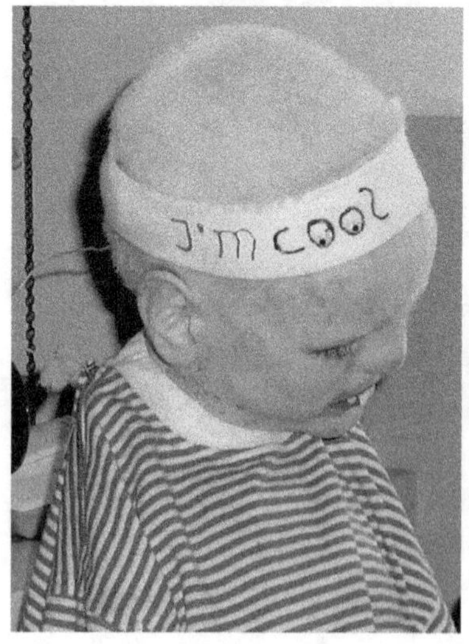

finally learned to let go of my 'perfectionism' – I did the best I could, and left the rest to God. How freeing it was!

We had high hopes with the cochlear implant, and were thrilled when we began to see results: when someone loudly knocked on a door, Na'il turned his head. Because he didn't like the magnet attached to his head, school came up with the idea of a bandana. It looked funny, especially after I wrote, "I'm cool!" on it.

All *shetel* children started off with a few 'hertz'; gradually, the sound ranges widened and the loudness increased. Na'il had started off with unusually loud sounds, which he handled very well.

As time went by, instead of adding sounds and frequencies to the Cochlear processor, the audiologist had to lower them even more. We began to wonder if we had done the right thing. It seemed as if his nervous system had become so sensitive, that even the smallest noise bothered him.

"Na'il is wrongly wired," we joked.

"You could be right," the audiologist responded. "It probably has to do with his syndrome. You never know, with these children."

And then, one day, Na'il simply refused to wear the *shetel*. The moment I put it on he wriggled it off his head. Afraid that one day he would lose the expensive gadget, we decided to give him a break. Perhaps we can try again at a later stage, I thought.

Thanks to the (expensive) Nutren formula, Na'il had grown taller, but this had also affected his already crooked spine. He was thin as a reed, didn't have a lot of muscles, and sitting, standing and walking must have cost him an enormous amount of energy. We noticed he had to rest more often and during school hours he lay on a bean bag.

Na'il continued to take our breath away!

Urit, his new teacher told us about his accomplishments: Even though he was deaf, he seemed to laugh at the right moment, and understood what was going on in class. We guessed it was because he was so perceptive, and able to read body language more than any other child. Na'il knew exactly which staff member worked on which day, and what the next lesson was. Without being able to utter a single word, he found clever ways to communicate; and his problem-solving skills... well, that was really something!

During school breaks, Na'il always wanted to go outside. One day he faced a real problem, because buggies and wheelchairs blocked his exit. Urit later told me how Na'il had solved this seemingly insurmountable problem. First, he observed the hurdles in front of him, and then looked at the door leading to freedom. With great physical effort, he then began to push each buggy and wheelchair aside, until he had paved his way to freedom. Urit had been astounded! Our little man surely took our breath away!

Why does he keep staring at the ceiling? I wondered. Na'il had returned home from school but he didn't rush to the bathroom as usual. Perhaps he sees angels, I thought.

"What do you see?" My heart stopped when I saw the lamp was hanging by a thread from the ceiling. The hook that secured it had broken off, and the heavy lamp could have crashed any moment on top of Na'il, who used to sit there watching videos.

"Oh! *Kol ha kavod!* Well done!" I hugged my little boy.
He smiled from ear to ear, obviously relieved that his slow witted mother finally understood what he had been trying to tell her.

Summer loomed, which meant the children spent lots of time at home. Na'il's upstairs 'bedroom' consisted of a corner with his bed and all kind of medical pictures taped to the wall. He reached it by sliding up and down the stairs via his back, or we had to carry him. I didn't like the idea that he was alone up there. Also for practical reasons I preferred him to be downstairs. If Na'il was hungry, he would 'holler' (make an "aaahhhh" noise) and I'd bring him his bottle. But he always had to go to the toilet afterwards, and then I had to run upstairs again to help him.
It was time for a major 'room-swap'. When Fahima was away for a week-long holiday, I set the plan in motion. Na'il received Fahima's room; she moved next door, and pushed Wim's study - annex guestroom into the sealed room. He now had to share space with our two dogs, while Nadia got my workroom at the end of the corridor. It was an enormous (sweaty) undertaking, but with satisfactory results for everyone, especially Na'il.
Now he could lie down on his bed whenever he wanted. He loved his new room, and I was glad to have him downstairs again.

Ever since receiving our temporary residency, Wim and I had been members of the Maccabi health fund. The children belonged different ones, Leumit and Klalit, which both were a pain in the neck. I spent many a frustrating hour waiting and fighting to obtain specialist referrals, often without results. Both girls now had reached the age in which they could choose their own health fund. To my surprise, Na'il could be added under my name. When all three children became members of the Maccabi health fund, my life became so much 'easier'. Referral headaches were something of the past, for Hadassah hospital, the place where we had our 'season tickets', was affiliated with Maccabi…. Ah, such bliss!

On September 1 Na'il began his last year in the Ma'ayan school. In a way, it saddened me, but we knew it was for a good reason that he had to move on – Ma'ayan couldn't teach him any further. This year was to prepare Na'il for new surroundings; he would learn to get used to different staff, and other children.

The Jewish New Year became extra special for us - we finally received our "Permanent Residency". The miracle had been helped along by our beloved neighbors, Zehava and Micha and the Ministry of Labor and Health. We never realized it would feel so different, but it did - we finally belonged! And they couldn't throw us out of the country anymore! The knowledge that our roots were firmly planted in Israeli soil took our breath away!

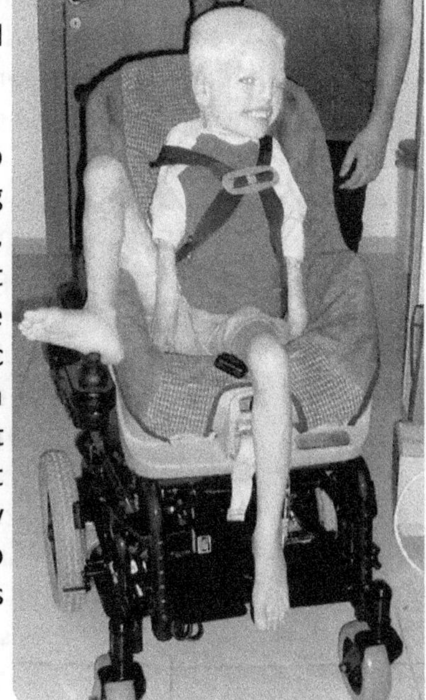

One day I answered the door bell to find Na'il's motorized wheelchair being delivered. They had forgotten to call us, so it was a pleasant surprise. Because it still lacked the insert, which had to be fitted according to Na'il's specific needs, I hid the chair behind a cupboard in Wim's study. Knowing that it would take ages before the insert was made, I decided to improvise by securing a car seat. Na'il was excited to find the chair in his room, and took his time to observe it from all angles.

Joysticks always held a special attraction to him, and now he had one of his own! Of course, he had to try out the chair, and we let him drive through the house to his heart's delight. It was a bit difficult to use the joystick with his foot, but he managed to get through the door without wrecking the place. His glorious, triumphant smile just took my breath away!

We had seen the announcements, but never thought much about it. It was Na'il who kept pointing with his foot to the Luna Park flyers. We found out that during the summer holidays, a mini Luna Park was set up behind the Teddy Kollek stadium.

The moment Wim took Na'il there he was hooked. Some activities were too dangerous for him but there were enough other things to be enjoyed with either Wim or Itamar. As the weeks went by, one youngster manning the booth took a liking to the enthusiastic little boy, and let him ride for free. Na'il loved every minute of it, the wilder the better. This wasn't Wim's piece of cake, but thankfully, Itamar could handle the whirling better.

Na'il refused to accept there no longer was a Luna Park. Even though Itamar walked all the way down to show Na'il the empty parking lot where his 'dream world' had been, he kept hoping that one day, it would re-appear. We felt sorry for our little boy and hoped that at least the motorized wheelchair could replace some of the fun he had.

Rosh ha Shana, the Jewish New Year was followed by Yom Kippur, Day of Atonement. This was the only day of the year that the roads, almost emptied of cars, were taken over by children on bicycles. Until then, we had not taken Na'il out in the wheelchair, because getting up the sidewalk didn't mean you would be able to get off again.

We didn't like having to walk on the road with cars zooming by with a child who wasn't used to his new chair yet. However, Yom Kippur was the perfect day for a trial run outside.

Na'il's face showed the exhilaration of the freedom to be outside and drive self. Even though his sitting position wasn't comfortable (he used his toes to steer the joystick) Na'il was insatiable and didn't want to stop. Wim and I took turns walking next to him, which sometimes looked more like running because Na'il preferred full speed.

He explored every nook and corner of our neighborhood, and for him the otherwise boring day became his most exciting holiday ever!
It was a pity we couldn't send him to school in the wheelchair. We had tried a few times, but the classroom was too small and the school not suitable for motorized wheelchairs. We just had to wait till next year, when he would go to Ilanot School. That had been one of the reasons I had pushed for a motorized wheelchair. This way, he was better protected against other children.
Being rather unstable on his feet, the slightest push caused him to fall. Rather dangerous for a child with osteoporosis. We noticed that when there were a lot of children around, Na'il anticipated possible bump-in's and always moved closer to the wall. The greatest danger was when he was taken off guard. In a wheelchair, he was mobile and safe, and for that reason Ilanot had been willing to accept him.

During Wim's Christmas holiday, we tried to put the "diversion principle" into practice and set out to explore the Old City of Jerusalem. This kind of outing was only possible without the children, and now we had this rare opportunity to see something new.
   "About time," I told Wim. "We're already 17 years in the country."
That day, we never got to the Old City. When I answered my mobile phone, it was Urit, the teacher. "Na'il has a fever," she told me. "Can you please come and take him home?"
This kind of unplanned 'diversion' was typical of our life.

Neither did we anticipate the snowfall. Like previous times, we ended up with having all the children at home. So much for wanting to use Wim's holiday to have some RR -'rest' and 'relaxation'.
But it was all part of our life, our ministry. The work we felt God had called us to do. Knowing and trusting that the Lord would give us the grace and strength needed to 'finish', we continued to run the race that was still ahead of us.
We went on, praying that the breathlessness we often experienced during this exhausting marathon, would be replaced by even so many moments that took our breath away.

16

A New School

In January 2007, another doctor was added to Na'il's favorites list:
Dr. Hasharoni, Hadassah's spine specialist. This wonderful, loving man immediately took a liking to Na'il. While the little boy sat on his knee the doctor checked him over, amazed by his lack of fear. People who, like this doctor, showed their compassion for Na'il, couldn't do any wrong with me!

"This little guy needs a spinal fusion," the doctor told me. "But first I want to talk about his multiple challenges with a team of specialists."
Our little boy was a 'special' case, and spinal fusions were long, complicated and dangerous. While talking things over the doctor permitted Na'il to freely roam his office, and open drawers with his foot. Na'il was as happy as could be!

The end of April I was asked to accompany Na'il once a week to visit Ilanot School. Before next year's enrolment the school wanted him to gradually get used to his new surroundings. When I entered the class I realized they were short-staffed, and because Na'il's deafness required extra assistance, I had no choice but to stay with him. Until the end of June, I spent every Monday from 8.00 a.m. till 1 p.m. in Ilanot.
Finally, Na'il could use his motorized wheelchair! He investigated every nook and cranny and explored the wide corridors and other classrooms. The teacher, a wonderful, patient woman, didn't mind a mother listening in. Na'il found it hard sit still and participate in his new class. The moment it was time for a break, Na'il continued his quest for new frontiers! It was very taxing on me, but it was the only way for Na'il to be successfully integrated next school year. On the other hand, it was a privilege to get a peek behind the scenes of a school day, and of getting to know these special people who, day in day out, faithfully worked with these very needy children.

The next morning I watched for Na'il's reaction when the next day I put him in his yellow buggy to go back to the Ma'ayan School. He accepted it but kept pointing to the pictures I had taken from his first Monday at Ilanot.

"Next week – again!" I signed to him.
He understood, and smiled.

May 27. Na'il's 13th birthday party a combined goodbye party from the 'hopeless cases' institution where he had learned so much. I realized Na'il was already 10 years with us!
The children wore the party hats Na'il always loved. Except for those silly paper hats (which he soon tore to pieces) there was hardly a toy (besides umbrellas) 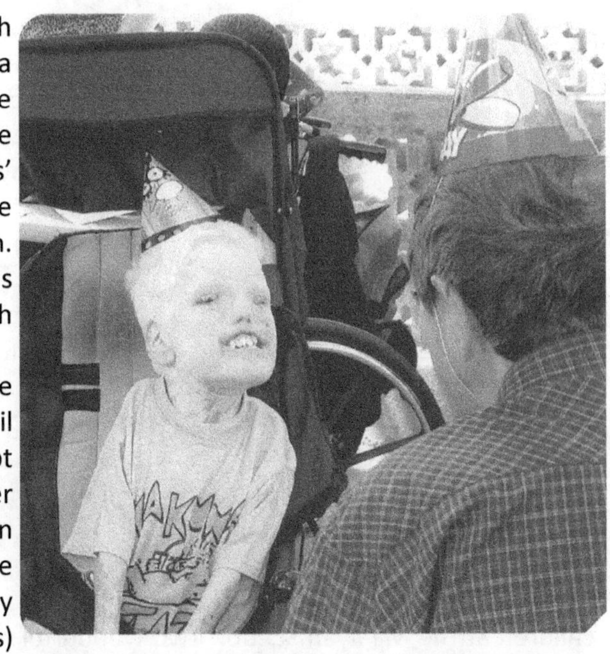 that he fancied. For him, those hats were like a special gift that brought him joy. Plain, 'regular' things could bring a smile on his face and he showed his enthusiasm by 'flapping' his arms. A new pair of socks lit up his eyes and he proudly showed them off in class.

Those Mondays in Ilanot weren't easy for Na'il either.
Two ladies, dressed as clowns, gave individual therapy to the children of his class. Na'il became angry when he wasn't allowed to join them. The next week, one of them gave him a big red clown's nose. But it wasn't the same one. Na'il wanted the clown's nose! In the end, he accepted his little red present. At home I put it on, and he immediately began to make funny faces in front of the mirror. I think he associated it with the dentist mask!

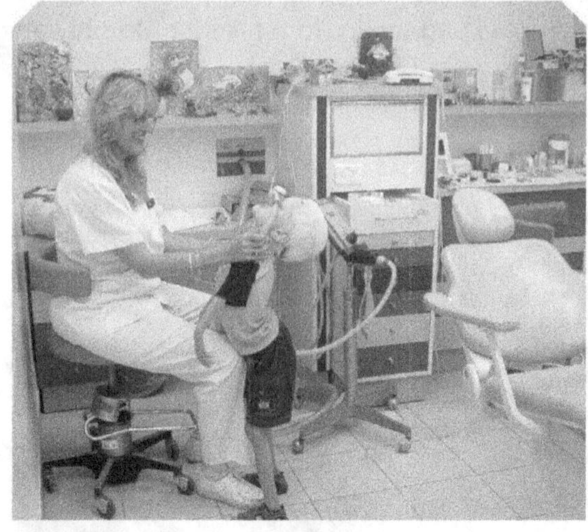

Even though he no longer needed the nitro during dental treatment, he still 'demanded' to wear the oxygen mask. Na'il favored Kathy's room, which was painted in soft colors and filled with pictures and little toys. He would take Kathy's hand and guide her to the oxygen tank with the mask, swinging his thin body with anticipated pleasure.

One day, while cleaning his teeth, Na'il protested.

"What's the matter? This doesn't hurt," Dentist Esti said.

"Did you open the oxygen?" I asked Kathy. "I think he doesn't feel the air in his nose."

Indeed, Kathy had forgotten to open the oxygen flow. Smiling happily, Na'il enjoyed his dental cleaning.

I felt sad for having to say goodbye to all those wonderful people and children at the Ma'ayan School. Two wonderful teachers, first Ora and then Urit, had been able to find the keys for unlocking Na'il's potential. Now, he had reached the limit of what they could further teach him. I was time to move to Ilanot.

Every school Na'il had been, there were girls who had a "crush" on him. Urit told us he was terrified of a girl in Ma'ayan, and with good reason. She was wild and rough, and could easily tackle him to the floor.

"But deep in his heart, he likes her too!" Urit laughed.

One day Na'il had kicked his girlfriend's shin, (probably out of frustration) which really hurt. He was stunned when she kicked him back. He never expected THAT! But it taught him not to hurt others, and he didn't do it again. It was so sweet seeing them together!

Professionals had been touched by Na'il's charm. I guess that's what attracted another girl, this time in Ilanot. Now I was the one who was afraid! While he gave his tired back some rest, the heavy, tall and clumsy girl moved her wheelchair closer to where Na'il lay on the mattress. Squealing with laughter, she took his leg and slowly began to pull. Na'il loved it, but I sat poised to prevent the situation from getting out of hand. But the two children bonded and had great fun together.

Ever since we sold the Hyundai, we had to make do with a Renault Cleo. Thanks to our new car, a Fiat Doblo, we now had room for a wheelchair and buggy, next to each other, without having to fold them. It was such an improvement! The Cleo's trunk barely had room for one folded wheelchair, let alone an additional buggy!

We struggled through a 2½ week long and for Na'il boring holiday. Finally, it was time to prepare him for the new school year.
    "You're going to Ilanot!" I pointed to the pictures.
Na'il became very excited.

Getting used to a new school wasn't easy, especially when it turned out he had a new teacher and different classmates. I wanted Na'il to roam around before he was cooped up in the classroom, so I took him to school early. Lena, the teacher's aid was already there.
    "You're working with Na'il's class?" I was thrilled.

When Nadia transferred from the Deaf school to Ilanot, Lena had made it possible for Nadia (for the first time in her life) to participate in a week-long school trip.

The dear woman didn't blink an eye when I explained Nadia's complicated care to her. From that moment on, Lena had become my 'star'! And now she was going to look after Na'il as well - what a blessing!

"I'm worried about his drinking habits," I explained. "He usually doesn't want to take his bottle from strangers. A dangerous 'habit', especially during hot weather."

Na'il rather went thirsty than accept help from people he didn't know or like. In Ma'ayan, he had allowed only two staff members to feed him. Nadia, the no-nonsense teacher's aide had been one of them. Lena seemed to be a similar type of woman.

"Give me the bottle," Lena demanded and before Na'il realized what happened she put the nozzle in his mouth and he began to drink. I was flabbergasted! "Leah! This is a miracle!"

That first school day was mayhem. The staff had to get to know the children, their needs, and the way they 'ticked'. The team of physiotherapists, occupational therapist, teacher and aids, had to search for walkers and contraptions for the children to stand in, often to find that the children had outgrown them during the holiday. I tried to pitch in wherever possible. It was awesome to see the staff's efforts to get the children back into their daily school rhythm.

During the two-week summer holiday, most parents either didn't have the energy or lacked the motivation to keep their children, most of whom suffered from Cerebral Palsy, in physical shape. It showed - the staff had to start from scratch.

I realized that I couldn't leave Na'il behind now. It wouldn't be fair to him, or the staff; they first needed to get everything in order and rolling, and only then would they be able to keep an extra eye on Na'il. He not only needed to get used to many new faces, but also to different rules. I noticed the much bigger school was rather overwhelming for him. He needed to adhere to very strict boundaries:

"No! You're not allowed to remove other children's joysticks from their wheelchairs!" and "No! You don't stick your foot in the toilet bowl!" Toilets held a magnetic interest for him; during the school break he visited each class to check them out for himself.

For 1½ long weeks, I returned home exhausted; but I knew it had to be endured in order for Na'il to succeed. Then one day, Ronit, his teacher said, "You don't have to come in tomorrow. I think we'll manage now." It was such a relief! Knowing that this sweet young woman would have a hard time with Na'il, I warned her,

"Be very strict with him at first. Later, you can take a softer approach."
However, she didn't heed my advice, and as I had feared, Na'il was rebellious and refused to listen. He kicked and screamed and even began to spit, not only in class, but also in the hasa'ah (school bus). Of course, he was overwhelmed by the new school and the big change that had turned his known world upside down. I wasn't surprised he couldn't handle it.
I knew that this (for us embarrassing) behavior was because he felt utterly frustrated for being unable to communicate what he wanted.
I felt sorry for him, and feared that people would only see his bad behavior, and not the special child that I loved so much, whom I understood.

After a few difficult months, slowly, gradually, Na'il began to cooperate a little. The staff too needed time to get to know Na'il. The school invited Urit and Nadia, his Ma'ayan teacher and aid, to tell the Ilanot staff how they best could work with Na'il. When everyone realized, they had to be VERY strict with him, things began to improve. He loved the class outings to the mall, except when they celebrated someone's birthday in a restaurant. One of the extra volunteers would then take him to the escalators. He couldn't get enough from going up and down. Because Na'il loved everything that vibrated, the staff began to use the vibrating pillow as a 'reward' for good behavior. It motivated him to 'work' in class.

Noah, the principal, presided over the first staff/parent meeting.
"I must tell you that we seriously thought of transferring Na'il to a different class. "She must have seen my shocked reaction. "Don't

worry. You know what the teacher and aids said?" She laughed. "We don't want to lose our Na'il! No way, Noah! What were you thinking?"

Referring to his behavior, they said yes, he was a challenge and often difficult, but they saw how special this little boy was and loved him. Hearing Noah (proudly so) speak about her wonderful staff, brought tears to my eyes.

"I can't tell you what a blessing this school is! For all of us!" I told the assembled staff.

Na'il's spitting behavior didn't improve with time. The child that happened to be sitting next to him in the hasa'ah (school bus) always had to bear the brunt.
School found a 'solution'- the bike helmet Na'il now wore on his face resembled a fencing mask. Because of his contractured arms, he couldn't remove it, so at least for now, the rest of the children were 'safe'. Even though Na'il was a difficult child in class and in the hasa'ah, at home he was as sweet as could be.
Often, Na'il's behavior was embarrassing, especially when he bit his teacher in her upper arm.
"We need to be sure Na'il isn't a Hepatitis-B carrier," Noah told me. His pediatrician ordered some blood tests, including the H.I.V. virus. Thankfully, all tests came back negative. All the 'worst-case-scenarios' that had been playing in my mind had been for nothing.

Na'il's infrequent visits to his biological parents weren't a success. Lacking secure boundaries, his behavior threatened to get out of hand. When Mahmud returned Na'il to our usual meeting point, he told us about his son's rampage.
"I think it's out of frustration that Na'il behaves like this," he said.
It touched me that he tried to 'soften' his son's behavior. "I think it's because you are too nice to him," I told Mahmud. "You need to be very strict. He needs to know who is boss."
Because they wanted to give their son a 'good time', he walked all over them. I had to learn to let go – outside my sphere of influence there

was nothing I could do about Na'il's behavior. I made an appointment with a psychiatrist. Na'il needed help and I had to get professional advice on how to deal with his obsessive and compulsive behavior.
God gave me the desire of my heart by fulfilling my writing dream.
I received Long Ridge Writer's Group's first diploma and began their next course – how to write a novel.
Writing brought comfort and relief, and could be combined with taking care of the children.

After all these years of giving, giving, giving, I now gave myself permission to write, without feeling guilty about it. Having arrived in my desired haven gave so much joy. I needed it!
Sandy Brooks, a wise editor friend once wrote: "Most of us writers start writing because we have a longing to meet a need deep within ourselves…. The Lord often uses our needs and longings to move us

17

Needs, Longings and a new Ministry

In 2008 I took Na'il for his first visit to the psychiatrist in East Jerusalem. The doctor remembered me from Nadia's hospitalization, several years ago. Na'il loved the doctor's room, which was also used by an obstetrician. The doctor prescribed a low dose of OCD (Obsessive Compulsive Disorder) medication, and warned that children like Na'il sometimes had opposite reactions. "We increase the dose very slowly," she said.
I pulverized Na'il's medication and added it to his milk formula, grateful he didn't seem to taste it. However, instead of subduing his compulsions and obsessions, the medication seemed to make them worse.

The operation to his spine was put on hold. I didn't mind, for I wanted Na'il to get used to his new school before an operation and long recuperation brought new turmoil to his life. His crooked spine must have caused him pain, but he never complained and found the most peculiar ways to 'rest'.

At the age of 21, Nadia had to say goodbye to the Ilanot School. At least we had another seven years to continue our love-affair with this wonderful school before Na'il turned 21.
That summer, Ilanot held a special *'Olympiada'* in which children competed against each other through games and exercises. As 'master' swimmer, Na'il had to 'race' against other children. He didn't have a clue what was going on, but enjoyed it tremendously because it meant more time in the pool. One afternoon he came home and motioned with his head to the rucksack hanging on the back of his wheelchair. Inside I found a medal and an award - he had won first prize for 'back stroke".
    "Oh! Kol hakavod! Well done! Mazal tov! Congratulations!" Hugging him brought a huge smile on his face.

During the two weeks that the school was closed, Wim stayed home to help with Na'il. We wracked our brains how we could keep him busy. Because of the heat and the fact that our little boy was only interested in physical activities, Wim took him to a pool in the Jerusalem Forest. It was the perfect solution and he loved it. The people were nice, and the (mostly Arab) life-guards were fond of the little boy. On the last day of the holiday Wim took Na'il to the pool in the community center, not far from our home.

"Why on earth didn't we think of this earlier!" he exclaimed. From then on, every Friday afternoon and Saturday morning Wim and Na'il went 'swimming' in the nearby pool. The long walks had always left us exhausted and him still full of energy. Now it was Na'il who came home tired. And satisfied.

On September 1 Wim and I met with a lady lawyer who set the guardian process in motion. It turned out to be a very expensive procedure, which we had to pay out of our own pockets. But with Na'il's future in mind, it was important to become his guardians. Only then could we apply for his handicapped allowance when he turned eighteen.

"If everything goes according to plan," the lawyer told us, "the whole procedure will take about six months."

Life slowly settled into a steady rhythm, and we noticed that Na'il's behavior began to improve. He was more relaxed, and when frustrated, he didn't spit, kick or scream as he used to do.

However, his obsessions and compulsions didn't seem to be affected by the medication. We tried to ignore them. During unguarded moments, Na'il somehow always managed to tear the rubber of his joystick. He stopped at the metal pin, which he couldn't remove. It made driving the chair rather uncomfortable, but at least it kept working. Because of his obsession to 'chew' the metal, his saliva ruined the electrical parts. The new joystick unit cost us a fortune. I won't let this happen again, I vowed and covered the new joystick with an (in my eyes) cleverly secured cap.

It proved not to be 'Na'il-proof'. He was obsessed with rubber, and from school we heard he had "chewed' all the protective rings

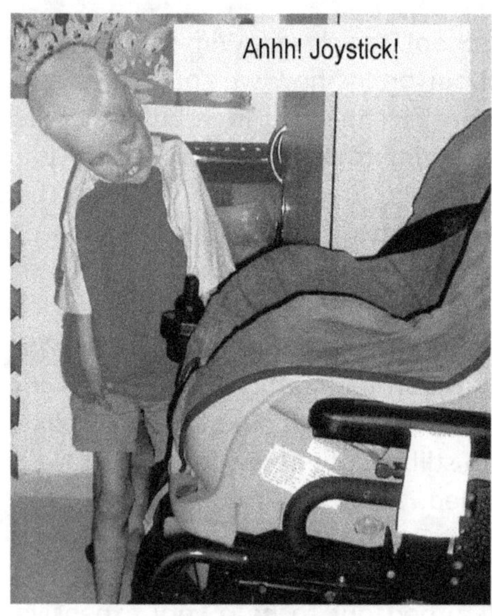

from the children's walkers. His new orthodontic braces, which had sharp metal pieces glued to his teeth, helped him to leave his mark on everything - "Na'il was here…."

Like many handicapped children, Na'il preferred a fixed schedule – he needed to know what to expect. We didn't mind that Shabbat was rather predictable as well. I'd wake him around 8.30 a.m. for if I didn't, he would sleep till 11 a.m. and refuse to go to bed in the evening. Wim took him to the pool for an hour, after which Na'il always wanted to go in the bathtub. "No. Later. In the afternoon," I told him again and again. Resigned, he'd then watch a DVD, and rest on his bed.

After lunch, when Wim went upstairs to take a nap, Na'il always 'posted' under the stairs. This way, he could keep an eye on the bedroom door. The moment Wim emerged he knew it was time for the Time Elevator. Na'il then raced to his room, as if the excitement that had been building suddenly had become too much for him.

During one of the holidays we had taken the whole family to the *Time Elevator*, which told the history of Jerusalem by going back in time. Na'il had fallen in love with the moving chairs, and the 3-D action on the screen. When Wim and Na'il became regular visitors, the staff began to recognize father and son.

"I'm amazed your son still likes it," one of the girls said.

Mad about it, was a better way of putting it, for he squealed in anticipation of certain actions; when the water scene came, he expectantly looked up, knowing there would be a soft spray of water coming from the ceiling. 'Jerusalem by night' was also a favorite. Then, little twinkling stars appeared in the darkened auditorium.

The Time Elevator was expensive, but we figured Na'il was worth every shekel - at least it was something he loved. Then one day, the girl behind the cash-register told Wim that from then on he only had to pay a special (very low) entrance price. We were touched by this unexpected act of kindness!

Wim didn't mind taking Na'il on these outings, but I began to worry about the future. He wasn't getting any younger, (61) and also suffered from osteoporosis. Heaving the buggy up and down the stairs to reach the pool, and lifting Na'il in and out of the car wasn't good for his back. Even though I was ten years younger than Wim, my energy level wasn't exactly what it had been. I dreaded the spinal fusion operation, which was still in the 'waiting' phase.
    "You must take things one day at a time," I admonished myself. "Trust the Lord to help us when the time comes. He will give us the strength we need in order to continue looking after our special children."

Na'il loved to go to school and the staff was enthusiastic about the changed boy. He now was motivated to work, and curious to learn new things. Lori, the occupational therapist, had long-term plans for our boy and tailor-made a program to work on his development.

I continued to write whenever I had the time. In the afternoon Na'il often crawled on his back to my upstairs study, just to be with me. It was a new area to explore, and he would get into all kinds of mischief. This didn't help my concentration, so I would take him downstairs for him to 'pester' his father.

Nadia was pleased to work at the social workshop; Fahima did her National Service in combination with a program which taught her to become independent. Much to our surprise, the Ministry of Health gave permission for two motorized wheelchairs. Na'il now drooled over two more joysticks! Nadia was afraid her little brother was going to wreck her joystick as well. Rightly so, for by now we were using joystick unit no. 3. Despite my efforts to 'protect' them, Na'il always managed to rip the rubber to pieces.

The infrequent visits to Mahmud and Sameera became more and more troublesome, even to the extent that Mahmud called me.

"Can you please come and pick Na'il up two hours earlier than planned? He almost wrecked our house."

I felt awful. Home again, Na'il was docile and happy and obedient. He knew his boundaries, and felt safe.

In November, I handed Na'il's prescription for 170 tins of milk formula to the health fund's pharmacy.

"We don't have it now," the lady told me. "We're waiting for a new shipment. There's no Nutren available in Israel and we don't know when it will arrive."

I was horrified. This was the worst-case scenario I hoped never to experience. I panicked, for Na'il was very particular with his food.

"Can you order a substitute?" I asked the pharmacist. "And what if he refuses to drink it?"

"You'll need another prescription."

My brain worked overtime. *Is the pediatrician in*? I wondered. *No, I need to talk to a dietician first. She must tell me what to give instead.* Thankfully, I had enough formula to last for another two weeks, but needed to act swiftly. It was an anxious time, but we found a similar formula, and to my immense relief, Na'il accepted the new 'brand'. He even seemed to like it better.

Someone informed us that every six years, handicapped children were supposed to undergo some kind of psychological testing. Na'il was curious to explore the center where they did the test. He especially liked the corridor that was built in a round-about way. While sitting in buggy, he tried to open all the doors with his foot. He went around in circles by pushing himself forward with his right leg. Running after him made me dizzy.

Waiting was never his favorite pastime, and it was difficult to keep him 'civil'. When the door of the psychologist's room finally closed behind us, Na'il immediately wanted out again. One look at the little boy, and the psychologist knew he would not be able to test him in the usual way. Instead, he asked me all kinds of questions, while Na'il impatiently kept trying to open the door.

Fifteen minutes later we were back in the hall, waiting for the next person on the list. The psychiatrist and I were surprised to see each other there. Her room was outfitted with a doctor's table, which at least kept Na'il happy for some time - he hoped for a check-up.

At the end of exhausting morning we met a group of professionals, who again asked all kinds of questions about Na'il. They immediately noticed he was a strong-willed, but curious and intelligent child. "Mild retardation", was their conclusion. The pediatrician wanted me to take Na'il to a gastro-enterologist.

"I want to know why he refuses to eat regular food."

Inwardly I sighed. "You know, I don't mind," I honestly told her. "Now I don't have to worry about his daily intake. If he drinks one liter, that's 1000 calories. Thanks to the formula he has become stronger. He's really a 'healthy' boy now."

Despite my plea, the doctor wanted me to see a specialist.

I was exhausted and Na'il cranky by the time we returned home - it had not been as much 'fun', as he had hoped it would be.

Mid December, I participated in a 'marathon' meeting in Ilanot, where I met everyone who worked with Na'il. Together we brainstormed how best to teach Na'il and what we should leave for a later stage. Again, I was impressed by their professionalism and motivation to help these very handicapped children reach their potential. Unanimously they spoke about their love for Na'il, the special boy they saw behind his outward 'weirdness', and the seemingly endless possibilities to teach him new things.

"You know Na'il plays the keyboard now?" the music teacher proudly said. "He used to bang on the keys to feel the vibrations, but I taught him to use his toes and play a melody."

"I know," I responded. "One of the orthodontists in Hadassah told me!"

This doctor and his wife happened to be friends with Na'il's music teacher, who had told them about the wonderful boy in her class. The world of the handicapped was a very special one! We felt so privileged to be part of it.

Just before Christmas, I updated the psychiatrist about Na'il's continuous obsessions. She told me to raise the dose to 250 mg.

Until then Na'il had not shown any of the possible side-effects. He was never sleepy during the day, and we didn't expect it to be different this time. I gave him the higher dose.

"Na'il was aggressive in class." I was shocked when I read the communication notebook. "When he didn't get what he wanted he toppled tables and chairs."

During school hours, he was sleepy, but at home he was his normal, sweet little self. We hoped his body would soon get used to this higher dose, and that the OCD medication would finally begin to work on his obsessions and compulsions, for which he needed them in the first place.

Sunday, December 28, while I was talking to our social worker, I got a worried phone call from Ilanot.   "Something is wrong! Na'il has fallen asleep in class," Lena, the teacher's aide said. "He doesn't have a fever, but we think the color of his legs is different than usual. Do you think we should let him sleep?"

Puzzled, but not overly worried I told her to wake him after an hour,

"Otherwise I won't be able to get him in bed tonight."

That afternoon Na'il went through the usual activities. He didn't seem different, or sick, and I figured the reddish color of his legs was because of the cold weather and his unwillingness to wear socks and/or shoes. Lately, when I dressed him in a pair of trousers, he immediately tried to wriggle out of them. If he didn't succeed, then, helped by his orthodontic brace, he first bit a hole on his knee and then ripped the trousers apart. In the end, I gave in and sent him to school in shorts, even in winter.

At night, he always slept with his legs uncovered, while his upper body was buried under a pile of blankets. When I woke him up in the morning, I was always surprised to find Na'il's feet were warm, and figured that he intuitively knew what he needed. When it wasn't hazardous to his health or too dangerous, I decided it would be better to go along with him.

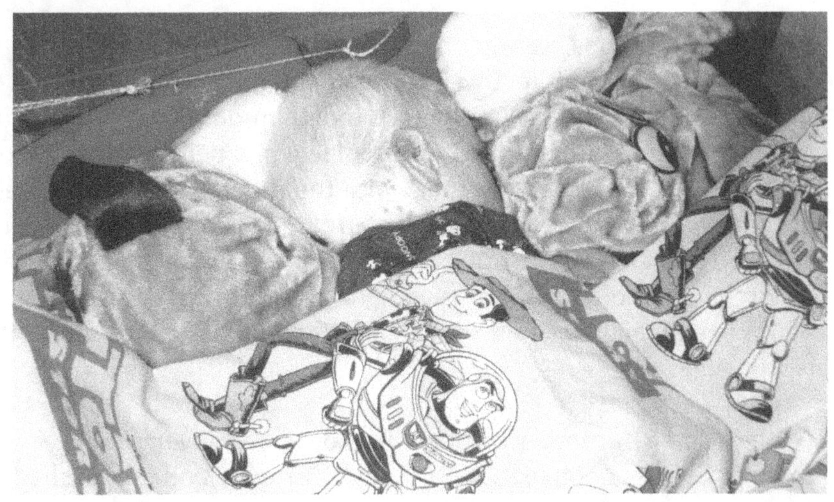

After having slept at school, of course Na'il didn't want to go to bed at his usual time, 8.30 p.m. To my chagrin, he kept me awake till 11 p.m. Expecting his body would get used to the higher medication, I asked the teacher to try and keep him awake during school hours.

Miriam arrived 'out of the blue''. Every Sunday afternoon she treated Na'il to fun outings. Last year, Miriam had been a student teacher in Na'il's class, and she had been crazy about the little boy.
At first, I wondered how he would respond to her, if he wouldn't act up, like he had done with Shimon, another volunteer who quit because he couldn't handle him anymore. Miriam turned out to be such a blessing, and Na'il loved her and accepted her authority. She was strict with him, and that was exactly what he needed. By bus she took him to the center of town, where he found many new areas to explore. The crown on those outings was always a visit to the Time Elevator.
Because we didn't want Na'il to go there two days in a row, we stopped the Saturday visits. Refusing to accept it, with his head he kept 'pointing' to the 'home activities' communication sheet which contained a picture of the Time Elevator.

Saturday afternoons, weather permitting I took Na'il for a walk.
One day he wanted to investigate a playground and noticed the swings. Unable to sit unsupported, I took him on my lap. He loved it, and I treasured his happy response. Holding him tight against my chest with one arm, I grabbed the chain with the other. He loved the feeling of the wind on his face, and the freedom he must have experienced as we were swinging to and fro. For parents with special needs children, playgrounds are always hard physical work. But the child's happy smile and squeals of laughter make the effort more than worthwhile.

By the end of December our best friends were moving, so we invited the team of helpers to eat at our house. For weeks on end we had lots of guests, which Na'il always loved. He often 'grabbed' a spoon from the table with his mouth and walked up to an unexpected 'victim'.

"What does he want?" the surprised visitor asked me.

"He wants to re-enact a visit to the dentist. You have to use the spoon to check his teeth!"
Speaking about obsessions!

It seemed the year had gone by quickly. I was tired, and attributed my restless feelings to the extra work and busyness that had come from helping our friends. Even though I couldn't place the feeling of foreboding, I didn't want to dwell on it. It must be the warning signs of another burn-out, I thought.
Would it have been that 'easy'. It turned out to be far worse!

18

Clouds of Sorrow

The year 2009 started very well for Na'il. On the first of January, Professor Becker glued the brackets on his lower teeth. I was grateful Na'il accepted the treatment and was cooperative - more than we had ever dared hope for! He showed off his new braces to everyone. The messages I kept receiving from school were still the same: Na'il wasn't his 'old' self.

I attributed his behavior to either the medication, his new brace, or the small infection on his outer ear. *It will pass*, I told myself. *We just have to get through this phase.*

Na'il was back to drinking his usual formula, Nutren, and I didn't see any changes in his drinking pattern or his stools. He always drank less in the winter and more in summer. Sometimes, when his growing body needed extra nourishment, he asked for more, only to return to his normal average of a liter a day. I had learned not to be anxious when he drank less, knowing he'd always catch up.

Mid-January the teacher wrote that Na'il slept for two hours in class.

I decided to lower the medication by 25 mg. to see if that did the trick.

Two doctor's appointments in one week made Na'il very happy! The lung specialist had to give the go ahead for a possible spinal fusion. Our special child amazed the two women doctors, and like a proud mother, I told them about his accomplishments.

It was impossible to check Na'il's lung-function, but they took my word for it that he could stay under water for much longer than most adults, and that he had never suffered from bronchitis or pneumonia. Just to humor him, Na'il received a physical check-up, which made his day.

Two days later, we were back in Hadassah to visit the gastro-enterologist. Waiting in the spacious lobby of the "Mother and Child" clinic was tough on Na'il. He kept nagging me to take him to the 4th floor - children's surgery – his favorite ward. I kept signing to him that he wasn't to have an operation today, but only a check-up. He refused to accept it and I was relieved when our turn came.

This doctor too was amazed and touched by the precious little boy. Na'il lay on the doctor's table, happily jumping up and down, ripping the paper to pieces. He tried to grab the otoscope (to check ears) with his foot. "Lo! No! Asur! Forbidden!"

I told the specialist about Na'il's lifelong habit of drinking only formula, and his subsequent growth and health. The doctor called a fellow specialist to look at Na'il. Both doctors checked and palpated his abdomen, listened to his belly, and concluded that it wasn't necessary to undergo all kinds of painful procedures to check why he refused to eat normal food. "You just continue with the Nutren," they told me.

Na'il was happy to see a group of doctors standing near the nurse's station.

"Hey, I know him!" one of the doctors exclaimed. "He broke his hipbone, wasn't it?"

"I'm amazed you remember him after all those years!"

"Could you tell me a bit about his syndrome?" the doctor asked.

Another doctor also showed interest, and grabbed a pen.

Like most Israelis, he had a hard time writing it down: "It is Klein…. What?"

"Klein-Waardenburg. Type three."

Most student doctors vaguely remembered reading about the

syndrome during their studies, but were always interested to meet such a 'case' in person. I was happy to share my knowledge with them, and Na'il loved the extra medical attention.

Next on the pre-operative 'to do' list was a visit to the anesthesiologist.

"She'll be in at noon," the kind nurse informed me. "Would you like to make an appointment for another day, or wait? I'll put you on top of the list."

I decided to wait. Feeling tired and hungry I had a hard time trying to keep a cranky, impatient child busy. He kept pestering me to go to the 4th floor and I began to regret my decision to stay. When we finally entered the anesthesiologist's room, the woman took one look at Na'il and barked, "I don't have time for you!" She moved some papers around. "You are lucky I'm willing to see you, but I can't help you."

Thankfully, she listened when I explained about the 'to-do' list. She looked at Na'il's file and gave me an additional list with things she wanted to have checked before such a major operation.

At least I didn't leave the room empty handed and was glad that it had not been a wasteful wait after all.

At home I had to deal with three urgent needs at the same time: Na'il had to go to the bathroom, the dogs were whining and yelping, they had to go too, and suffering from a hunger-induced headache I was ready to crash.

Like always, a mother's needs had to be put on hold. Na'il couldn't be left alone, so I took him along to walk the dogs, who then needed to have their 'dinner'. Of course, Na'il needed another bottle, and only then, Mom was able to look after her own, suppressed needs. While Na'il played in the bathtub, I crashed on the couch where I slept with one ear and one eye open. After ten minutes Na'il often managed to climb out of the bathtub and I didn't want him to be running around cold and naked.

Psychiatric medication usually took three weeks to kick in, so I knew that lowering the dose would take time before we could expect to see results.

At school, Na'il continued to be restless and agitated; he often fell asleep in class and seemed to have a short attention span. But his appetite was normal and so were his stools. In the afternoons and on Shabbat, Na'il didn't seem to be different and I figured his need to rest more often was because of his disfigured spine. By now I had lowered the dose even further, back to the previous 200 mg.

The psychiatrist was surprised to hear about Na'il's seemingly strong reaction to the higher dose and frowned when I told her about his aggressiveness and the fact that he often fell asleep in class. It was a strange reaction indeed. "But you never know with these children," she said.

Nadia was the first to come down with the flu and passed it on to Na'il. Thankfully, he 'only' had a fever, without vomiting or diarrhea, so I treated his high temperatures with the usual medication. After a few days, he was well enough to return to school.

Thursday, January 29. During the monthly orthodontic check-up, the professor proudly showed his colleagues how well Na'il's teeth responded to the braces. Our little man basked in all the attention, was more alert and I noticed he smiled more often. I hoped he was on the road to becoming his old self again.

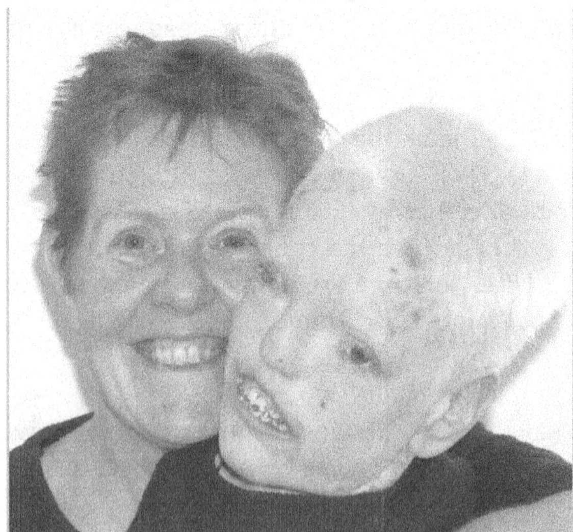

"We have been putting it off long enough," Wim said. "Let's take some pictures of the two of us."

That Saturday, January 31, I used the self-timer to take a series of pictures. Na'il always wanted to look through the viewer, and just for fun I grabbed him to take a few shots of the two of us.

But he wasn't interested in having his picture taken - he wanted to peek through the camera.   Later, I regretted that I didn't use the opportunity to take a picture of Na'il's reaction when he saw the print-out. Bubbling with laughter, with his big toe he kept pointing on my face in the picture, flashing a glorious smile in my direction. He didn't understand the phenomena, but it made him so very happy. Little did I know it was to be the last picture of our beloved son.

Sunday, February 1st.
Na'il coughed when I took him out of the school bus and the driver's aid told me he had been asleep during the whole trip. Na'il seemed tired, but didn't have a fever, so I let Miriam take him to the Time Elevator. It turned out to be his very last visit. They returned home earlier than usual, and according to Miriam, Na'il had been very tired, not his usual self. He wanted to go into the tub, and that evening I found he had another fever. It was the flu season and everywhere I heard people suffered from coughs, vomiting and diarrhea. He's still weak from his previous bout of the flu, I thought. He must have caught it again.

Monday, February 2.
Knowing I would be stuck at home with Na'il, I headed for the nearby mini-market to stock up on food. As I walked downhill, the crisp morning air tingled in my nose. I almost tripped over a stone when I greeted a woman who was on her way back after her early morning walk. The security guards of a Knesset member living in one of the apartment buildings in our neighborhood just finished checking the parked cars nearby. Another guard stood in line at the cash register.

"Great you're open so early," I told Chaim, the store owner. "In Holland they only open after 8.30 a.m."

"Same in Belgium?" he quipped. "Over there, the shops open only after 9.30 a.m. Nice and easy, relaxed, no need to hurry." Chaim had been up since 5 a.m. and his work never seemed to end. "It was boring to live in Belgium," he confessed.

"I can image," I told him. "In Israel, everything seems to happen at once. Never a dull moment in this country! May your day be blessed Chaim!"

"Amen!" He responded. "Same to you!"

The smell of freshly delivered bread lingered in my nostrils. The bags pressed heavily on my shoulders as I slowly trudged up the hill. Up in the grey and baby-blue sky, dotted with some fluffy clouds I spotted three white ibis, flying in lazy, steady formation. Probably spent the night in the Biblical Zoo, I thought. There was the sharp call from a pair of green parrots who were on their way to the park. The sound of hammering from a building site gave a steady rhythm to the music of the morning, filled with bird song. The rising sun began to paint Jerusalem's stones with a warm glow.

I sighed deeply. It was such a privilege to live in Jerusalem! On the neighborhood's sand-stone hills new shoots popped up everywhere. The gnarled almond tree beckoned the bees with its first white flowers. I took one last deep breath of the fresh morning air and stepped inside our house, where Wim stood ready to leave for the office.

"Na'il's awake." He kissed me goodbye.

It wasn't easy trying to explain to our little boy that he couldn't go to school because he was sick. I settled myself for another day at home, grateful to have at least had this 'morning experience'. "Don't despise the day of small things!" the Bible said. I tried to.

Na'il's fever was high and he had diarrhea, but at least he drank regularly. I hoped it wouldn't get worse than that, and we'd end up in hospital again.

Despite the temperature Na'il was alert, he wanted his usual bath and watched a DVD, although he slept a lot in between waking periods. That's good. I thought. Sleep is the best medicine.

That evening we went through the usual bed-time ritual. While lying on the dresser, I brushed his teeth with the electric toothbrush he loved, then cleaned between the metal brackets on his teeth. This was finished off with injecting some mouthwash he let stream out of his mouth, onto the double towel under his head.

He never tired of this twice daily ritual; our little boy loved to be taken care of, this treatment of his sensitive body. He loved it when I massaged him with body lotion, and his face with Nivea. His dry eyes needed artificial tears, which he thought was exciting.

A night-diaper, then pajama shorts, and our little boy was ready for bed. I'd lift him in my arms, cuddle and kiss him and put him in bed.

In the past, Na'il used to turn from side to side during the night, but now only slept on his right side. I guess it was the most comfortable position for his crooked back.

Tucking him under his pile of blankets, (legs exposed) always had to be done in a certain order with his favorite one on top. After one last kiss on his forehead, I stroked his short cropped, silvery white hair and left the room.

That night I slept restlessly, worried about our little boy, and prayed the fever would break. I attributed the sense of foreboding to my fatigued mind and body.

Tuesday, February 3.

Na'il's fever was still high, his stools looked like diarrhea, and he slept a lot. Because I already had an appointment with our pediatrician, I decided to take him there, despite the fever. He was alert and happy to go there, although he lacked the energy to roam around.

The kind doctor listened as I described the symptoms, and confirmed that many children had come down with the flu. She prescribed an antibiotic ointment for the small wound on his ear. To appease the little boy, who lay expectantly on the doctor's table, she listened to his heart, lungs and abdomen, and couldn't find anything wrong with him.

"Just make sure the fever doesn't get too high," she advised. "For the rest, let nature take its course."

It had been an intensive day. Even though I was bone tired, I decided to go for a walk around the block to get some fresh air. When I came home Na'il made gagging noises. He often did this when snot slid into his throat, for he couldn't blow his nose. Could it be from his coughing? I wondered. Although his temperature had gone down a little, he seemed restless.

"I'll sleep downstairs," I told Wim. "I'll be close by in case he really gets sick."

An hour later, Na'il's restlessness increased. He seemed out of breath, his belly looked inflated and felt hard as a rock. Something was very wrong!
Emotionally detached I went through the motions and prepared a 'hospitalization' bag. My fears were confirmed when our neighbor Micha, a doctor, listened to Na'il's abdomen and couldn't hear a sound.
Looks like an ileus (blocked intestines), I thought. *After the operation, he'll be all right. We just have to get through this. God help me, for I'll be in for a long and sleepless night. If not weeks!*
In my already exhausted state I dreaded the prospect, but there was no other option than to take our precious boy to Hadassah Hospital. Fast!

Dress rehearsal

19

Into the Father's Arms

9.30 p.m. Sitting on the floor in the back of the car I held Na'il's buggy while Wim drove us to Hadassah Hospital. Na'il sat up straight, and I think he realized we were going to his favorite place, but he was too busy trying to breathe to enjoy it. Wim had to return home because we couldn't leave Nadia alone. In the Emergency Room's children's department, we soon were directed to the intensive care corner. Na'il's health quickly deteriorated. I entered a living nightmare.

He stopped breathing when a nurse tried to insert a tube into his stomach. It seemed ages before the anesthesiologist managed to intubate him and attach him to a respirator. Several nurses and two doctors tried to stabilize his rapidly failing blood pressure. Nobody could tell what caused the deterioration. They only knew that Na'il's belly was filled with air.
Because many children suffered from flu complications, the department was filled to overflowing. Nurses from the adult department had to assist. Parents are usually not allowed to stay while medical staff works on the child, but because they knew I was a nurse, they let me become 'part of the team'.
Only after Na'il's blood pressure (which was so low, they could hardly find it) was stabilized, a CT. scan was made. Noticing the color of Na'il's legs, in my heart I knew we were fighting a lost battle. According to the CT. scan, the major organs were surrounded by air, cutting off the blood circulation to his kidneys and legs. There was no sign of a perforation, and nobody knew what caused the air to accumulate in his abdomen.

An Arab doctor called Mahmud, who arrived at the same time as the pediatric surgeon. One look at the little boy and the surgeon sadly shook his head. Na'il was dying.

"There may be a 1% chance that an operation can bring relief," he said. "But it's possible that Na'il dies during the operation."

Mahmud wanted to take that 1% chance, but I knew it was already too late for Na'il.

Wednesday morning, 4 a.m.

While Na'il was operated on, Mahmud and I anxiously bided our time in the empty waiting room near the operating rooms, waiting for the world to wake up.

6 a.m. An exhausted surgeon brought us the sad news he had not been able to help Na'il. Necrosis of his small intestine, probably due to a blood-clot, caused the creation of gasses. For an hour, the surgeon had tried to close the wound, without success – the swollen mass could not be put back into the abdominal cavity.

Na'il had survived the operation, but we had to wait and see if he would be stable enough to be transferred to the ICU on the children's ward.

The hospital woke up, the morning shifts began to arrive, and we waited for news of our precious Na'il. Wim arrived at 8 a.m. surprised to find Mahmud and me still waiting near the recovery room. The morning shift had not known we were still there. Pediatric surgery on the 4th floor of the children's wing had always been Na'il's most favorite place. Now he was in I.C.U. without realizing it.

Mahmud, Wim and I were ushered into a room, where two doctors, a social worker, the head nurse and two other staff members gave us all the time we needed to ask questions. They listened to our stories, and then prepared us to say goodbye to a dying boy.

Hooked up to even more wires, tubes and drains, Na'il's face already had the color of death. His blood pressure was almost nil and his pulse very low.

On one side of Na'il's bed two of Mahmud's brothers stood crying. I sat down on the other side, stroking his face, his short-cropped hair, kissing his already cold forehead, his closed eyes, the beautifully formed ear that never heard, all the time trying to imprint his beloved features before it was no longer possible. Wim and I said goodbye to the precious child - a 'one-of-a-kind-gift' from Heaven.

"Go towards the Light, Na'il," Wim released him.

As the life of our beloved boy ebbed away, I remembered a poem from Jan de Hartog, who compared dying to the sailing away of a ship.

"Death is like the departure of a ship. At sunrise, she unfolds her sails and makes for the horizon. When the ship disappears behind the horizon, everyone will stay behind sad. But somewhere, at the other shore, a group of people will be eagerly waiting. And when at a distance, they view the sails, someone will very happily cry out: "THERE SHE COMES!""

9.30 a.m. The doctor and a nurse approached the monitor near the bed. "Time of death: 9.30," the nurse said while the doctor turned off the ventilator.

Because of the machine, we had not realized he had died.

Our beloved Na'il's soul had gone to Heaven, welcomed in the waiting arms of our Heavenly Father and those who had gone before us. Now he was free from his broken, fragile body, which he had left behind in the bed. We tried to picture him running and laughing and talking! And then looked at the white, still figure in the bed and cried.

On the one hand, I felt sorry that Sameera, Na'il's biological mother, had not been there; on the other hand I was grateful, knowing that I would have been compelled to comfort her and in doing so would have lost precious last minutes with Na'il. Wim and I had been able to say goodbye and cry over our child together, in peace.
It was a privilege to help the nurse wash and clean our boy one more time. I asked her how Na'il was transported to the cemetery.
   "Usually the parents take the child in their own car," she said.
I was shocked! Such a thing was difficult to comprehend for us Westerners. After one last kiss, the body bag was closed, and I was never able to see or hug or look after our 17 kilos, precious little boy any more. He died in his most favorite ward!

Immediately after the confirmation of Na'il's death, the administrative wheels for the funeral arrangements were set in motion. In Israel, people must be buried within 24 hours, and for Mahmud it became a race against the clock. We were grateful not having to deal with the burial arrangements and I asked one of Na'il's uncles if his body was to be transported by ambulance.
He looked shocked. "Can't we take him by car?"
I then realized he was thinking about the cost this would involve.

Mahmud didn't have a clue what time the funeral would take place.
   "I wonder if you will be able to find your way around on the Temple Mount," he told Wim. As women were not allowed to attend Muslim funerals, Wim decided to let it be.

I stared after the body bag containing my precious boy until the door closed and the auxiliary nurse took him down to the hospital's mortuary. It was time to say goodbye to the wonderful staff on the ward. The I.C.U. head nurse hugged me tight and wished me strength. Exhausted from the ordeal, utterly sad and still in shock because of the suddenness of it all, Wim and I walked back to the hospital's parking lot.

Around noon we came home with a buggy, bags, and no child. Na'il's school and our social worker had been notified while we were still in the hospital. When I called Ilanot they had been in the middle of a joyful happening - an "open day" for the neighborhood, anticipated and planned for a long time ago. While there was merriment and joy in the main hall, in the headmistress' office people cried and were in shock when they heard our sad news. They were resolved to keep it a secret until the program had finished. The news that Na'il had died, was received with unbelief and more tears.

While I tried to get some sleep after a sleepless night, Wim called his family and our neighbors. The previous night, after Wim had dropped me off at the hospital, he had sent out emails to our worldwide friends, asking them to pray for our little boy. Now he had to tell them the sad news of his death. Soon, from all over the world the shocked reactions began to arrive. The trickle grew into an outpouring of encouragement, comfort and love.

Our social worker was with us when we told Nadia the news that her 'brother' had died and now was in Heaven. She burst into tears, and a few minutes later sniffed, "Can I have his room?"
I heard a car stop in front of the house and looked at the clock - 3.30 p.m., the time Na'il usually came home from school. His driver and aid came inside for a minute to give us a hug and to cry with us. Never again would we hear the honking of the bus, announcing Na'il's arrival from school.

At 4 p.m. Mahmud phoned with the news that Na'il had been buried in the family grave behind the Temple Mount, opposite the Mount of Olives. Wim's eyes were drawn to the calendar hanging on the wall, depicting that same area.
With increasing astonishment, I listened to Mahmud's tale of the burial. After obtaining the necessary permit from the Ministry of Health, the hospital handed over Na'il's body to Mahmud.
He first took him home so the women could see him one last time. Then they raced to Jerusalem's Old City, to be in time for prayers on the Temple Mount.

After the ceremonial cleansing, which, due to the way Na'il looked after the unsuccessful operation must have been gruesome, the men assembled for prayer.

When the worshipers in the Mosque of Omar heard Na'il had been handicapped, the atmosphere changed. Muslims believe that a handicapped child has a 'clean' soul, is without sin. Thus, Na'il was an angel. In order for them to reach Heaven as quickly as possible, angels had to be brought hastily to their grave.

While holding Na'il's body above their heads, instead of walking sedately to the cemetery, the worshipers RAN. Carrying an angel was a great honor, and the men fought for a chance to touch him.

Mahmud was pushed aside and had to run after the funeral crowd.

At the family grave, another scuffle erupted; this time the men fought for the honor of putting Na'il in the family grave. To Mahmud's chagrin, he had not even been allowed to bury his own son. That honor was bestowed on his father and another man.

We shuddered while trying to imagine what that burial must have been like, and were grateful Wim didn't attend. Mahmud promised to take us to the grave one day – we wouldn't be able to find it because everything was written in Arabic.

"Is it true that Muslims believe that handicapped children are angels when they die?" Wim asked a man called Mohammed a few weeks later. He said it was.

"But why then do they see the birth of a handicapped child as a curse from Allah?" Wim wanted to know.

Mohammed didn't know how to respond to such a difficult and for him probably forbidden way of reasoning.

As Christians, we believed that when Na'il's heart stopped beating, his soul was taken up into Heaven, welcomed by his Heavenly Father. The child left the shell of his disfigured body behind, which eventually would turn to dust.

Christians believe in the second coming of Messiah. Jews also wait for Messiah to enter Jerusalem through the Golden Gate, opposite the Mount of Olives.

That's the reason why there is a Muslim cemetery in front of that Gate - they know a religious Jew will never set foot on a Muslim cemetery. But... they'll be in for a surprise when Messiah returns to the Mount of Olives. Our beloved Na'il has been given the privilege of a front-row seat!

Even though we were not Jewish, we decided to have a seven-day mourning period, the so-called Shiva. For the Jewish people this begins after the funeral.
That afternoon I didn't have the energy to cook, and Wim's colleagues blessed us by bringing a casserole.
Somebody else gave us a pot with fragrant hyacinths and a beautiful card, from which I copied the motto, "Grieving a loss, Celebrating a life".

Together with our closest Dutch friends (who had become like family) we cried and mourned the loss of our precious little boy.
More e-mails poured in, and the phone didn't stop ringing. Because my Hebrew was better than Wim's, I had to tell the whole story over and over again. I put Na'il's bedding and clothes in the washing machine and made some order in his room. It was so hard to imagine that he was not coming back. Ever.

That night we rolled into bed, exhausted, and woke up at 3 a.m.
Slowly, the truth began to filter through my sleepy brain, until it hit me again. I lay there, crushed, overwhelmed by grief and the feeling of loss, wetting the pillow with my tears.

Waiting for morning to come.

20

SHIVA Blessings

Thursday, February 5 - Day 2 of the *Shiva*

Nadia's appointment with the psychiatrist couldn't be postponed. She was in dire need of professional help, even more so after this traumatic event. Wim drove us to East Jerusalem. The same doctor had been treating Na'il, and as the tears streamed down my face, I told her what had happened.

"If you ever need to talk about Na'il," the dear woman said before we left, "you can always make an appointment."

At the office, while Wim collected everything he needed to mail the Embassy's newsletter from our home, one of his colleagues saw me waiting in the car.

"You know what I keep thinking?" She wiped away the tears. "Na'il enjoyed the 'ultimate' time elevator. He went straight into Heaven!"
It made me laugh and cry at the same time.

"Can I please come over to your house?" Miriam wrote in a SMS.

We began to see the importance of the Shiva. It would be good, not only for us, but also for others who had loved and known our little boy.
I presumed the dentist's secretary had heard about Na'il, but she only called to change an appointment. She was shocked to hear what had happened. A little later, Professor Becker called to express his sorrow with our loss. Then the dental department's head-nurse called.

"Can we please come and visit you?"

Zehava, our neighbor, explained how one goes about a *shiva*, what the rules were and what was expected from family and visitors.
We decided to have 'open house' from 10 a.m. till 7 p.m.

After my sister in Holland had told my eighty-eight-year-old mother in person about Na'il's death, we cried over the phone together. Even though she had not seen Na'il since her return to Holland, he had always been *Savta's* special little boy. There were so many precious memories of the two of them together.

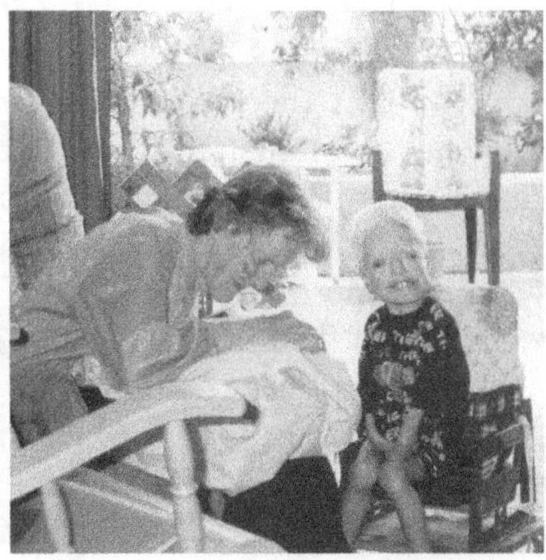

I worried about my mother in faraway Holland, wished that she was with us, able to share the outpourings of love and comfort we received. And of course, my mother worried about me, wondering how I would cope with this loss

Visitors didn't greet us with the usual shalom, but with "I'm so very sorry", and the first thing they did was grab a photo album. Nobody wanted to eat or drink something, just to sit with us and remember a precious boy.
We were touched by the shared memories, and moved and awed by the special way 'our' boy had touched so many lives in the almost twelve years he had lived with us.
There was hardly time to breathe, let along cook a meal during the day. I was grateful Wim's office provided another casserole. My appetite was gone, but it was a blessing for the rest of the family.

Another short night followed. Again, I woke up at 3 a.m., assaulted by the knowledge there was no little boy waiting for me in the morning, no child who needed my help to get ready for school.

Friday February 6 - Day 3 of the *Shiva*
Six days a week, around 6.30 a.m. I would wake Na'il by gently stroking his soft, short cropped white hair and kiss him on the cheek. Now I was sorry that I never took a picture of his funny way of sleeping with his legs exposed. This morning, Nadia woke up with, "Na'il's dead. Can I have his DVD's?" Thank God for simple souls!

In order to remember Na'il's treasured memories, which so easily could be forgotten in the grind of daily life, I began to jot things down.
People often asked when I was going to write a book about our life in Israel. I had thought about it, but wasn't ready (yet) to write about the living hell Moshiko had created. We didn't have too many precious memories of the ten years he had lived with us.
Na'il however, had been a totally different child. Even though we had sacrificed a lot because of him, most of our memories were special, happy ones. My website became a platform, and the stories I wrote were filed in a blog called, "Celebrating a Life".

I thanked God for my gift of writing. Without it, I surely would have been completely lost, staring into an enormous hole. By putting Na'il's memories into words, I could channel my grief in a constructive way. Added to that, I also wanted the world to know what a special child Na'il had been. This way, I hoped he would continue to minister, even after his death.

People visited our house, called and wrote us. Even though at times it overwhelmed me, we were so blessed by the concern, encouragement and love. One of Wim's colleagues cooked a chicken casserole and made a chocolate cake, only because Nadia had told her that she loved chicken and chocolate!
I wondered what the Shabbat would bring. The idea filled me with trepidation.

Saturday, February 7 - Day 4 of the *Shiva*

We were still trying to come to grips with the sudden and unexpected loss. Na'il's precious memories and the love of so many dear people sustained us. It also comforted us to know that Na'il was in the best place he could be - Heaven!

That Saturday morning, instead of taking Na'il to the nearby pool, Wim hung up the announcement on the notice board, and told the frequent swimmers what had happened.

The house felt quiet. Too quiet.

"It's as if Na'il is away, visiting his parents," Wim said.

In the pleasant afternoon, he almost suggested taking Na'il for a walk.

There was so much to get used to. Until that fateful Wednesday, our Shabbats always revolved around Na'il's needs and activities. The helpless child needed our help to drink his bottle, go to the bathroom, then into the bathtub, then watch a DVD, then Wim took him for a walk, etc. No longer would we hear the impatient 'rattling' sound Na'il always made with the toilet seat, his sign for having to use the bathroom. Fast! No longer did I need to quickly save my writing and run downstairs to help him. Now we had plenty of uninterrupted time to 'relax' and read or write, something we always wished and hoped for, and learned to do without. The "one day, perhaps?" kept our dream alive. Now that day had arrived and we didn't know what to do with it. The many pictures of Na'il helped us to remember the stories behind them. There were so many precious memories!

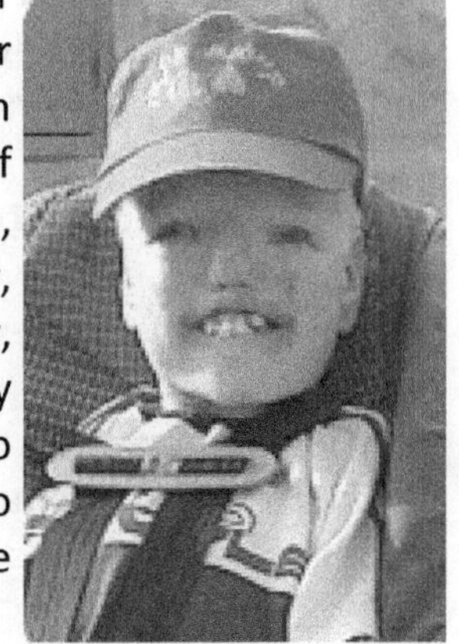

When nobody showed up that Shabbat morning, we were grateful for the unexpected rest. In the afternoon, we had Dutch visitors.

One couple worked with mentally and physically handicapped children near Bethlehem, and the woman, a nurse, worked with Russian immigrants.

I had been wondering what to do with the 170 tins of formula we just bought for Na'il and now the answer had come to visit us! We donated Na'il's formula and his diapers to our Dutch friends who passed them on to others in need.
Again, I was amazed at the *Shiva's* rippling effect. It was such a blessing – for us and others. Only a few days later did we find out that because Shabbat (the 'Queen') should be a day of joy, on that day people usually didn't visit a house in mourning.

"Shavua tov! Have a good week!" we wished each other that Saturday evening, the beginning of a new week.
My eyes were still red and swollen, but the crying had become less. *Is that normal?* I wondered. Sleeping was still difficult, and it seemed 3 a.m. became my normal waking time. Physically we were not tired, but felt exhausted, emotionally in particular. We felt carried by the prayers being said on our behalf. God was with us in a special way.
For me, sleepless nights usually meant migraines. Never before in my life had I been forced to talk so much (in Hebrew!), and rack my brain to find the right words. That too would have been a headache trigger. But none came. Another miracle!

Sunday, February 8 - Day 5 of the *Shiva*
"You know, now we will be able to go away for a weekend," Wim suggested. "We can even take the girls to Holland for a long overdue holiday."
Hearing him say that, I wanted to run and hide. That was the last thing I wanted to think about! Being in survival mode, I wasn't ready to think about the sudden 'possibilities' Na'il's death had brought.

It seemed as if a dam had burst that Sunday morning. Visitors came, wave after wave after wave. There were teachers and principals from the Ilanot and Ma'ayan school arrived. Ilanot gave us a disk with pictures from the special display they created in the main hall of the school. Some children had posted letters and drawings on the board, and a memorial candle burned next to Na'il's picture. It brought tears to my eyes.

There were also many phone interruptions, "Just wanted to make sure you are all right…." I then went back to the visitors and talked, explained, and shared some more about a very special boy.

My voice was almost gone because of all that talking in Hebrew, and we had hardly time to eat, let alone drink something. I was glad when it was 7 p.m. After a short walk around the block to get some fresh air, I longed for my bed and inwardly groaned when I saw Wim talking to one of our neighbors. Only now she had heard about Na'il's death. Even though me legs trembled from fatigue, I gritted my teeth and talked some more. When I finally collapsed in bed I prayed for strength, wondering if I could survive another day like this.

Monday, February 9 - Day 6 of the *Shiva*
God knew what we could handle. That day, we still had visitors, but thankfully, they only came in two's and not one after the other. We continued to share and talk about Na'il and showed the many pictures.

"The first three days of the shiva are those of the deepest grief," a religious neighbor explained. "These are usually spent with the closest family members. On the fourth day, the grief is still there, the loss too, but the tears become less."
Hearing this explanation, I felt relieved. My way of grieving wasn't strange after all.

Another Dutch couple visiting us said they needed to move. We could help them find another house - the *Shiva*'s ripple effect….
When there were no visitors, Wim kept busy sending and answering e-mails; I worked on Na'il's blog, and wrote stories. It triggered an overwhelming avalanche of ideas.
A friend invited me to post a story about Na'il on her blog. Titled "A Beautiful Boy", it received encouraging comments.
I know how I'm going to spend the Shloshim (30 days of mourning)! I thought. *By writing about Na'il.* But there was a price attached - in order to give it all my attention and energy, I had to put my new novel on hold.

Our lives had changed drastically. I was aware that I needed to give myself grace. I needed time to work through this loss, and should not embark on new 'missions'.

Only one more day to go. I was exhausted, and wanted it to be over already.

Tuesday, February 10 - day 7 of the *Shiva*

Was it only one week ago, that Na'il was still alive? It was so incomprehensible, so difficult to grasp. However, the raw truth didn't lie - his empty room; the motorized wheelchair, unused in a corner; Na'il's dressing table filled with photo-albums. An umbrella on the bed – which, had he been alive, wouldn't have lasted longer than five minutes. We no longer needed to lock the medicine cupboard - a door he always checked first thing in the morning. When I forgot to lock it, he always peeked inside the drawer, ready to steal a syringe.

"Oh, you naughty boy!" I'd quickly lock the door.

With twinkling eyes, he would squeal with laughter, as if he wanted to say, "Got you, *Ima!*"

The memorial candle next to Na'il's photos on the sideboard was lit one more time. I was glad the *shiva* was coming to an end.

Wim and I thought back on the week that was. Here we were: a Christian couple, sitting a (Jewish) *shiva*, for a Muslim boy - our family in a nutshell. This *shiva* had been such a blessing for us: the outpouring of love, comfort and encouragement from so many friends, neighbors and acquaintances had been overwhelming. It had really helped us to begin processing our grief.

We had experienced the wisdom of this Jewish ritual, which you read about in the book of Job - the story of his so-called friends who came to visit and 'comfort' him. That was an example of how NOT to do it!

There was so much to be thankful for! It truly had been seven special and blessed days! And now, with the grief less intense, but nevertheless still there, it was time to get on with life!

21

The Little Prince

Thirty days after burial Jewish people hold a so-called *Shloshim* - a special ceremony. They usually meet at the grave for the unveiling of the tombstone, say Kaddish (prayer for the deceased) and remember their loved one. We asked Noah, Ilanot's headmistress, if we could have a memorial service at the school. It took place on Sunday, March 15, and turned out to be a touching and precious event.

Na'il's classmates had taken his sudden death very hard and only now began to find their bearings. The staff felt it would be better for the children not to participate in the rest of the program.
The teacher, Ronit, read from a booklet the children had made in honor of their classmate. These very handicapped youngsters, each in their own special way, expressed their sorrow in losing their friend.

Ronit wrote her own story in Hebrew. This is the translation:
"Na'il ~ I remember the first time I met you, 1½ years ago. That was on the first day of the new school year. At first I was worried and startled by you. I resolved to be your teacher and to love you. Very soon, I got to know the person you are, your special charm, and got to love you. It was a special challenge to teach you – your progress was constant, and I never knew what next you would be able to learn. You added joy to the class and your naughtiness and your pleasure and you always surprised us with your creativity. You found things in school that gave you pleasure, things to enjoy, like e.g. a walker, the big saucer, an electric toothbrush, even 'eating' joysticks! You found amazing ways to get where and what you wanted; in a special and creative way.
It's so difficult to imagine you're no longer with us, for you were a child full of life, full of action and vitality. I love you and miss you! Ronit, your teacher during the last year of your life at the Ilanot School."

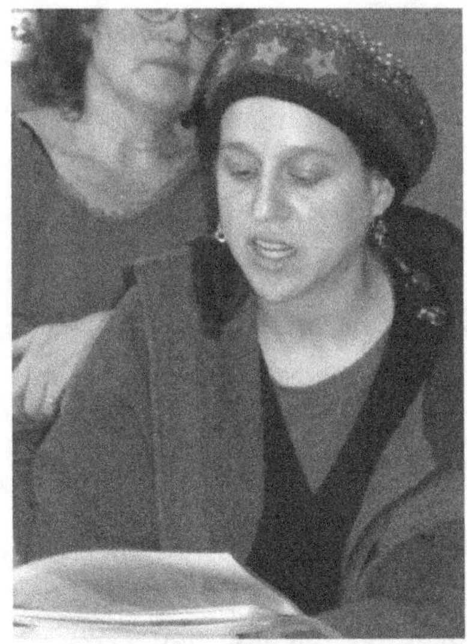

<u>נאיל-</u>

אני זוכרת את הפעם הראשונה שפגשתי אותך לפני כשנה וחצי.

זה היה ביום הראשון של שנת הלימודים.

בהתחלה, קצת חששתי ונרתעתי ממך.

תהיתי לעצמי כיצד אוכל להיות המורה שלך ולאהוב אותך.

אך מהר מאוד למדתי להכיר את האדם שבך, את החן המיוחד שלך
ולאהוב אותך.

זה גם מאוד מאתגר לנהל איתך ואנה התיחסתי לכל התסריאה

פעם לא ידענו לצפות מראש עוד הצליח לימוד.

בספת לכיתה שמחה ממעשי השובבות שלך ומההנאות שלך ותמיד

הפתעת אותם ביצירתיות שלך

מצאת דברים מעניינים בבית הספר שמהם אפשר להנות ז"לעשות

חיים", כמו: ההליכון, הצלחת, מברשת השיניים החשמלית, המנוף

ואפילו אכילת הג'ויסטיקים.

ידעת לנהל בצורה מדהימה את עצמך ולהגיע ליעד שאתה רצה

בדרכים מיוחדות ויצירתיות.

קשה להאמין שאתה כבר לא איתנו כי אתה היית ילד של חיים, מלא

אקטיביות וחיוניות.

אוהבת ומתגעגעת

רשות המורה שלך רשעה האחרונה לחיוך בריות הספר "עולים"

Wim and I wiped the tears from our eyes and hugged this wonderful woman.

The room in the basement was crowded with staff members and a few older children.

Noah began by reading an excerpt from the Hebrew translation of *The Little Prince,* written by Antoine de Saint-Exupéry. When I later read the English version on the internet, I appreciated her reading the story even more. Noah often had to pause and swallow her tears before she could go on. She ended her speech with:

"You too, Na'il in your own way, were a little prince. You taught us so many things during the short time you were with us. You taught us to love you very much, you taught us so much about the will to want something. You often had great joy. You taught us happiness, and showed us that it could be found even in the small things, something that we, grown-ups don't always succeed to remember and to do. You found ways to tell us what and how exactly you wanted something, and you pressed on until we understood what you wanted. And then there was nothing more wonderful than to see your triumphant smile! You taught us Na'il, that inside that little body of yours, was a little prince with a great soul, and lots of joy and love for life!

In the 1½ year you were with us we saw you grow and develop, you learned and did many new things, got to know others, and learned to love them, and also to listen to the staff who worked with you with great love. You had special relationships with Ronit, Sylvia and especially with Lena who loved you so much! And you continued to be the curious and naughty Na'il, who wanted to explore and investigate everything around him. You added life and color to the school. Anew we got to know Wim and Petra better, their great heart and love gave you many good and happy years and love without end. And to give you the best possible life. And now, we all have to miss that...

It's already a month now, Na'il that nobody races through the school corridors in your little yellow chair. Already a month that nobody lies in your green bean-bag. Already a month that we didn't see your glorious smile. A month that we miss your curiosity, your naughtiness, your joy for life.

And sometimes, Na'il, at night, when I think about you and look at the stars, then I smile, because I know that up there, you sit on your own little star, the one you already had time to explore and get to know. I'm certain it's already full of wrecked umbrellas, and rubber that you chewed up, and many swings that await you. Or a giant Luna-park, and the whole day you can do just what you love and want. And it's good for you over there, you are happy and laughing all the time. And please, send us your glorious smile, so we won't feel so terribly sad.... For then Na'il, I won't be so very sad, as the little prince said, - "And so it will be as if all the stars were laughing, when you look at the sky at night... And you will sometimes open your window, so, for that pleasure... and your friends will be properly astonished to see you laughing as you look up at the sky! Then you will say to them, 'Yes, the stars always make me laugh!"

I loved you, Na'il, and I miss you, my little prince! Noah."

There were not many dry eyes after this moving expression of love for our little boy!

Another teacher had made a beautiful short film/slideshow, which clearly showed Na'il's love and enjoyment of life. His smile could be so glorious! How I missed my little guy!

More speeches followed: a teacher's aide expressed her admiration and love for Na'il; one of the children wrote a 'song' about him and said he hoped it would encourage us when we were sad. The children, most of them suffering from C.P (Cerebral Palsy) spoke with difficulty, but tried to express what was in their hearts. It was so precious!

Of course, Wim and I were expected to say something as well. We expressed our gratitude to the assembled staff.

"You are so special!" I told them. "The work you do in the lives of these children is just wonderful. The dedication and love you have for these special children, the often-hidden potential you try tried to expose, can't be expressed in words." I looked at the people I had come to love and admire. "Thank you for the privilege of having been part of a team; together we have worked to give Na'il the best life possible."

Trees symbolize life for the Jewish people. Throughout Israel, the holiday of *Tu B'Shvat*, the New Year of the Trees, was celebrated around the time of Na'il's death.

Yuval, a teacher planted five trees in the school's garden in memory of Na'il - an Oak, Terebinth and Judas tree.

On our way home Wim and I mused on the fact how blessed we were by the love and warmth of the Israelis.

They were not ashamed to share their tears with us, or to express their sorrow for the precious child who made such an impact in the lives of those around him.

Na'il had been such an example to us 'healthy' people, and was sorely missed! His memory was truly blessed, and that treasure nobody could take away from us!

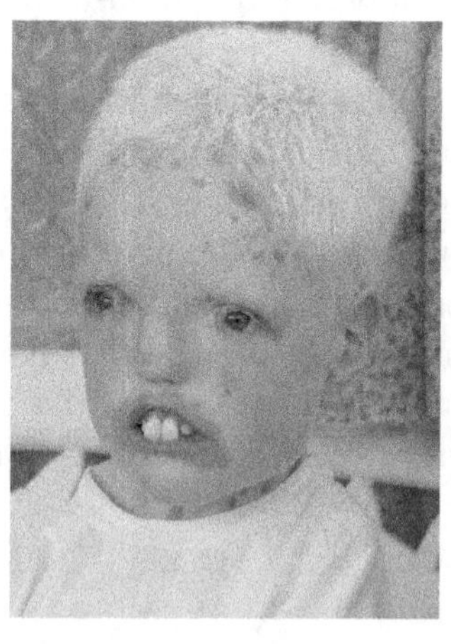

22

Finding Rest in God Alone

Na'il, of blessed memory, continued to be part of our new way of living. However, it still felt 'weird'.
Nadia got her wish, and was happy with the smaller room that had been Na'il's. Our subsequent 'spare' guestroom was soon filled with visiting friends from abroad.

After reading "Good Grief", a booklet about the ten stages of grief, (see bibliography) I knew I had to give myself 'grace', especially because I was quickly overwhelmed by seemingly minor situations. I had to learn to leave my worries and anxieties, my 'What next?' questions for what they were, and to rest at the bosom of my Heavenly Father. It wasn't easy, but an important part of the grieving process.

Just before Na'il died, I had been on the brink of another burnout, and the emotional earthquake his death caused, didn't help much either. I needed some extra 'time-out'. God's Word promised that I could come to Him, weary and burdened, and that He would give me rest. By taking up His yoke (not what I added to it), He promised that I would find rest for my soul.

"God had planned something better for us," (Hebrews 11:40)
I knew that the Lord, in His time, would show us the plans He had for us. Our girls still needed us to care for them, so we still had a long and demanding course to run. Most of it took place in the trenches, without applause, but we were determined to go on, towards the goal: "…. If only I may finish the race and complete the task the Lord Jesus has given me…" (Acts 20:24.)
We now could do other things, and I had more time to write. There were times, while I was writing this book, that I couldn't handle the emotions that were released. It wasn't easy to go back into time, to re-live (by reading our old newsletters) the hardships and struggles we had gone through.

Remembering those difficult times was tiresome, and I wondered how we had been able to survive the seemingly endless challenges, problems and crises. But the overall picture clearly showed God's hand, mercy and sustenance amid everything. I grudgingly had to admit that those problems always had been opportunities for growth.

As I put my feelings, frustrations and emotions on paper, the pain and longing for Na'il, I noticed it really helped me deal with my grief.

Wim and I felt privileged to be part of Israeli society, where there was room to mourn. A few weeks after Na'il's death, I met some people who didn't frown when I burst into tears while telling them about Na'il. They weren't embarrassed, didn't look for a way out, nor were they at a loss on how to respond. Instead, they listened with empathy, which means that they felt my pain in their heart. When it was appropriate, they even hugged me.

In Israel, mourning is a 'normal' part of life, not something that is hushed up, or ignored and perceived as something you do in private. The Western world can learn a lot from the Jewish people!

Our God is a God of comfort. He often worked through people who understood how we felt, what we'd been going through, or were struggling with. They had been there, gone through a grieving process, and had come out stronger.

> *"Find rest, O my soul, in God alone;*
> *my hope comes from Him.*
> *He alone is my rock and my salvation;*
> *He is my fortress, I will not be shaken...*
> *He is my mighty rock, my refuge.*
> *Trust in him at ALL times...*
> *Pour out your hearts to him,*
> *for God is our refuge."*
> **Psalm 62:5 -8 NIV**

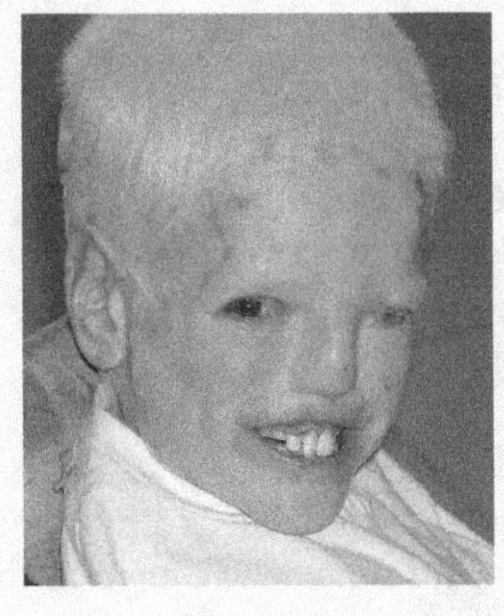

Na'il didn't have to do
anything to 'earn' our love –
we loved him for who he was.
Sent to us by God,
he wasn't precious
because of the things he did,
but because
he was precious in God's (and our) sight.
The value of his person
wasn't measured by his usefulness -
in the eyes of the world
he was a financial 'burden'.
In a world that is obsessed with
productivity and strength,
filled with people who look down on weakness
and scoff at deformity,
God used Na'il as an example.
He was the echo of God's eternal love for us.
And for almost twelve years
we had the privilege of taking care of him.

23

Grief's Important Journey

**"If you recently suffered a crisis, trauma or major loss,
give yourself grace; give yourself time to process the pain,
and give God time to restore your bearings."**
Pam Vredeveld

Wise words, but so difficult to put into practice!
God's word doesn't say we should not grieve, but that we must not grieve like those who have no hope. Knowing the answer beyond the grave comforted us, but we still had to go through our own, unique, personal grief journey.

Deeply entangled inside me were intense, draining and often unpredictable emotions. There was fear, pain, loss, sorrow, apathy, confusion, anxiety, sadness, dread, anguish, helplessness, disappointment, depression, dismay and lack of control.
The intensity of those ever-changing emotions left me disoriented, forgetful and feeling overwhelmed. Sometimes I was ashamed about my weird reaction to something seemingly trivial.

The floundering emotions made my life a roller coaster ride. At times, life spun out of control, and I grasped whatever handle I could find to hang on. Fighting for control made me so tired, and depleted my recourses.
"Rest in God", those words kept coming back, but that too was something I found hard to do while struggling with 'restlessness'. I felt exhausted from 18 years non-stop caring for multi-handicapped children, and having to deal with one crisis after another. I felt like a tightly coiled spring, ready to snap. How I longed for inner peace.

"Grief distorts our perception and requires a tremendous amount of emotional energy. There is little left over for anything other than mere survival." Pam Vredeveld

It was a tough nut to crack for someone like me who always felt the need to be 'productive'.

Streams in the Desert gave me a handle to hold on to. "God asks us to wait before we go on so we may fully recover from our last mission before entering the next stage of our journey and work."

Diarrhea, triggered by the anxiety, worry about the future, together with the strong emotions that grief had released, added to my stress and discomfort. Until I read that stress and trauma influenced the serotonin levels in the epithelium lining the gastro-intestinal tracts. It also affected my immune system. No wonder I had a hard time getting rid of that nasty cold and cough. Knowing why I suffered from all kind of 'weird' symptoms relieved my anxiety, and eventually the diarrhea spells stopped.

During the *Shiva* I had experienced that tears were God's healing balm. Dry-eyed I now could talk about Na'il to people who didn't know him. However, when I met those who did, I turned into a weepy willow.

It seemed as if I was suspended in time with the hours and days passing in slow-motion. Later I learned this was because my senses were (temporarily) numbed in order to gradually come to grip with my loss.
Na'il's death made me realize how 'small' I was, how fragile life and 'happiness' was. It had ripped me apart on the inside. He had been such a part of who I was, and now I had to find my identity back.
But how? I didn't feel our life's ministry was over yet. Should we take in another child? I lacked the physical strength for that. Should we 'retire' and rest on our laurels?
What do You want us to do, Lord? I prayed.
"Rest!" was the answer that kept coming back.

It wasn't enough. I felt the need to DO something, to FIND something to fill my long, 'empty' days. The idea of an 'open-ended' future filled me with dread.

Except for working on Na'il's story I couldn't concentrate on any other writing. Lacking the motivation, inspiration and joy, my new novel was indefinitely put on hold.

Anxiety and restlessness tossed me around. It drove me nuts. Grief's unexpected turns took me two steps forward, and one step back. Even though I was impatient to 'get it over with', all I could do was allow my grief to run its course.

"Perceive each new day as a challenge, a test for your courage. The pain will come in waves, some days worse than the others, without any reason. Accept the pain. Little by little you will find new strength, a new vision, born from that same pain and loneliness, which at first seemed impossible to be processed."

Daphne du Maurier's word helped me to see things in perspective.

I got more insight in the mourning process by reading the book "Through a Season of Grief". It spoke of the need to work through the grief, and not trying to get around it. Entering the dark tunnel of grief meant that I was on my way out – no matter how long that tunnel proved to be. And the light at the end of that tunnel wasn't the light of the oncoming train – it was the light of God's hope!

Grief's timing wasn't mine. Unexpectedly, it could jump on me. One moment I said I was feeling fine; the next I was sobbing. The seemingly lack of control was frightening and unnerving.

And then, in July 2009 the request came to take in another multi handicapped child. The hope infusion gave me a handle to hold on to, it was something positive to investigate, to pray, think, ponder and dream about. Our ministry obviously had not come to an end. True, we still had 23-year-old Nadia living at home, but it would only be a matter of time before she would move out too.

Light had broken through the oppressive somber clouds. My heart felt lighter too. Now there was room for other things and I could channel my energy into productivity instead of feeling drained by doing 'nothing'.

"Let's take our time, at least till the beginning of 2010," Wim wisely suggested. We were still in mourning, and shouldn't rush the process.

Six months already? Isn't about time we should get on with our lives?
Only six months? I'm not ready yet!

Because we are human, we all experience loss, which doesn't always have to be through death. It could be the loss of a job, or someone else getting it, a move, a pet, a friendship. Not having dealt with past losses would accumulate, intensify and complicate the new loss.
Writing down my personal losses triggered an avalanche of emotions and the intensity of those deeply buried emotions cost me a lot of energy. Grieving surely was 'hard' work!
I compared it to a deep physical wound. Mine was deep and complicated (because of the burn-out) and I needed to give my exhausted body and emotions time to be replenished.

Gradually, I began to venture out more, always glad to return home, where I felt safe.
Reaching out to those who also grieved taught me that, in order to come out 'whole', it was important to complete the grieving journey.
A couple who lost their teenage daughter in a traffic accident, became frozen in their grief. Even though they had another child and even grandchildren, to them life had lost its goal and purpose. They continued to exist, but without joy and fulfilment. I felt so sorry for them!
There was a widow whose husband had been the center of her life, and he had always taken care of her every need. When he died after a short illness, her life was 'over'. All she saw was a gloomy future of growing old alone, while her only son was busy with his own life. Her family lived in another city and her in-laws were only interested the money of her husband's business. What a hopeless future.
Believers may experience a similar situation, but when we make Christ the center of our lives, he will take our hand and give us the daily strength we need to live out that day. In Him, we have a future and a hope!

October 2009

Doubts invaded my heart. *Is it really your will, Lord, to take in another child?* I dreaded the idea of the renewed rushing, the stress, the crises that surely would come, the physical strength I would need to care for a physically handicapped older child. I felt depleted of strength – the price I paid for having walked on my toes for so many years. God knew our hearts, our willingness and our limitations.

Lord, I need an answer! I prayed. *We must decide – yes or no. I can't go on like this. I'm willing, but feel I just can't do it anymore.*

The answer came through a belated reaction to our newsletter.

"For many years now I've read your newsletters, and I'm under the impression that for a long, long time you've walked on your toes. I think you should take a very long time to get some rest. Most probably, the Lord has something else for you to do, something that physically isn't so taxing. And your writing ministry – shouldn't you take time to do that as well?"

It was true. I longed to spend more time on my writing. The simple version of Na'il's book "Just Do It" began to touch people's lives, and I knew God wanted me to use the talents He had given me.

Thank You, Lord, for giving me this answer.

Peace returned when we made the decision not to take in another child. Had we heard wrong? Had it been our imagination or personal longings?

I believe that God used the 'request' to lift me out of the pit of despair. My view was broadened and we had become open to new adventures. It had turned me around, helped me back on my feet, and had given me renewed hope and energy.

No harm had been done to the child, who had been unaware of what was going on.

We were grateful for not jumping right in, that we had taken our time, and followed the advice of our social worker to go slow. For a change, we had been able to keep the 'secret' to ourselves, and didn't talk about it with others, except for the people involved.

We knew we were entering a new season of our life. Our financial security didn't have to depend on the care of another foster child. God would provide – we had to trust Him for that.

February 2, 2010 - Na'il's *Yahrzeit* – the first anniversary of his death. My mouth fell open when I opened my devotional Wisdom for the Way by Charles Swindoll. "Celebrating Life!" was the theme of that day – the same we had chosen when writing about Na'il's life. Psalm 90 was awesome too.

Wim and I knew we had come a long way since that fateful day in February 2009. While we continued to treasure Na'il's precious memories, life went on.

After grieving a loss, we will never become our 'old' self again. It's a long process, but eventually I hope grief's journey will equip me to help others who are facing similar tragedies. I know my faith in God has become stronger, and in a way, I have become 'stronger' too. God can use our brokenness to help others heal. To let others know there is hope.

So, when you are grieving, and someone tells you there will come a time when you will go 24 hours without thinking of your loss, from experience I can tell you it's true.
What I've also learned is that while going through a time of grief you don't want visitor's delivering a 'sermon'. All you need is a listening ear or a shoulder to weep upon. Grief must be released, not suppressed.

We need people who can relate and support us as we go through our journey of grief. How badly we need them. How few there are! We can set an example.

What comfort to know that we are not alone on Grief's Journey - our Heavenly Father will never leave, nor forsake us. As Wim often held our little helpless boy in his arms, likewise, we may find shelter with the Rock of Ages, our eternal Refuge.

He is our strength and shield.
In Him we may rest.
Like a child, safely in the arms of his father.

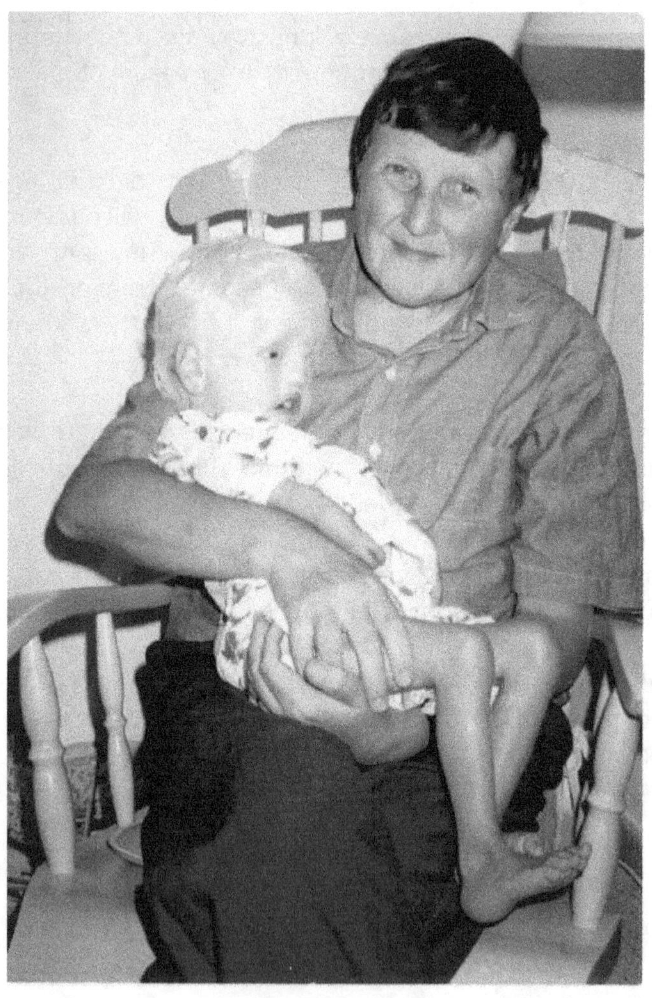

Ten Stages of Grief

Adapted from the Booklet Good Grief, by Granger E. Westberg

These stages usually occur randomly, not specifically in this order.

1. Shock – God's way of helping us to face the grim reality bit by bit.
2. Emotions – crying is one of them. We must allow ourselves to express our emotions – it will help the healing process.
3. Depression – part of 'healthy' grief. It feels as if something has come between the sun, you and God. It will pass – the sun is there, even if you don't see it.
4. Physical symptoms – Psychosomatic symptoms often appear when people don't work through their grief.
5. Panic attacks, inability to concentrate, fixated and obsessed by the loss. Wallowing in your gloom will prolong the grieving work.
6. Guilt – is a normal reaction. "I didn't do enough," or "I shouldn't have said this or that," etc.
7. Anger and resentment – looking for someone to blame, a scapegoat to vent our anger and pain.
8. Resist returning – frozen in grief. Refusal to remember your loved one, warts and all. Idolizing the deceased, making him into a saint.
9. Hope – the dark clouds begin to break up and rays of light come through.
10. Affirming reality - even though the struggle continues of learning how to live with the loss.

Grief's Many Steps

1. Acknowledge and understand your grief. Admit it and talk about it.
2. Identify your needs – physical, emotional and spiritual. Communicate your needs to others and allow them to help you in a concrete way.
3. Grief in your own way and at your own pace – you and your pain are unique.
4. Talk (or write) about your grief. You need to do so in order to experience healing. Slow down and let grief run its course.
5. Even though it hurts, chose to continue the grief journey. Only then you will be able to finish the course. You need to commit yourself to this journey.
6. Reach out to others who grieve, and you will be comforted and blessed in return.
7. God will prove Himself true in your life, if you let Him. (Proverbs 3: 5,6)

The importance of a 'good cry'

"What soap is for the body, tears are for the soul."
Jewish Proverb

According to scientists, crying is a natural way of releasing toxins that are associated with 'good' and 'bad' emotions. Stressful tears contain ACTH, a hormone associated with high blood pressure, heart problems, ulcers and conditions related to stress. Trying to keep emotions at bay or suppressing them, sooner or later will lead to a volcano-type explosion. Putting a lid on them will only cause the pressure to build up inside. When the explosion occurs, it may have become uncontrollable. Denying yourself the need to cry will delay the healing journey.

Weeping removes toxic substances that build up during emotional stress. It also reduces the body's manganese level, a mineral which affects mood. Certain chemicals, built up during stress and removed by tears, actually lower stress. These include a certain endorphin which helps control pain. Tears reduce tension, remove toxins and increase the body's ability to heal itself.

Weeping often occurs when we are unable to fully verbalize complex, overwhelming emotions – they water the soul.
♦ "The silent language of grief " - Voltaire
♦ "To weep is to make less the depth of Grief" - Shakespeare,
♦ "Tears are the safety valve of the heart when too much pressure is laid on it." - Albert Smith
♦ "Tearless grief bleeds inwardly." Christian Nevell Bovee
♦ "Crying often makes us feel better, even though the circumstances haven't changed a bit."
♦ "Tears are God's gift to us." Rita Schiano

We should have a 'good cry' more often!

Before we were to meet our new handicapped foster child for the first time, the social worker warned us we would receive a shock.
She was right - we did experience a jolt, but then looked past the passive, empty-eyed child laying on the floor and saw a precious human needing love and care. He was only three years old and had been through so much already. His young parents couldn't cope with his multiple handicaps, and saw him as a curse from God. Na'il was born with a rare combination of two syndromes, part of them deformed facial features.
The first time we could take him home for a visit, the little deaf and dumb boy immediately felt at home. The three older special needs children that made up our family accepted him like one of them, and even the dogs were happy to put up with him.

Through the years, against insurmountable odds, Na'il grew into a mischievous, often smiling boy who amazed everyone by the way he tackled problems and found a way to 'tell' what he wanted.

Our other children were dark haired and their skin brown tinted, and people often remarked that Na'il was the only one who looked 'like me'. He was partially albino, with white hair, a very fair skin but blue eyes and a radiant smile. To me it was a compliment, and proof of God's grace, working in the life of this special child.

We saw his beauty, his sweet character and precious soul, but were often rudely reminded that his outward appearance could trigger a gasping response. People sometimes turned away in shock and disgust, while children screamed and ran away. When that happened, we were grateful Na'il was deaf and at least couldn't hear those responses.
But we, the professionals who worked with him and the people who accepted him as he was, saw him like a lovely flower lending its sweetness to each day.

Na'il touched the lives of those he met in a kind and gentle way, just by being himself. We live in a world where people spend thousands of dollars on facelifts, diets, body enhancement and trying to look 'perfect'.

God however, has a different opinion.

In Samuel 17 we read how the people of Israel expected King Saul's replacement to be a 'film star' type of man. But the Lord had young David in mind, and Samuel told the people in verse 17: "The LORD does not look at the things man looks at. Man looks at the outward appearance, but the LORD looks at the heart."

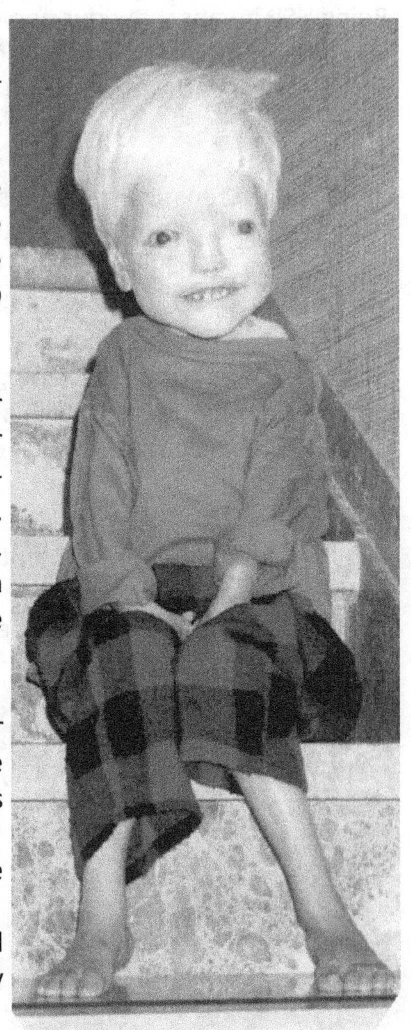

We've noticed that people who either worked with special needs people, or had them in their family, always approached our boy with an open heart. He immediately responded to them. Sometimes, brave, curious children asked what was wrong with him. He liked them too.

I felt sorry for the people whose fear for the unknown made them miss the blessing of getting to know a precious soul.

All they had to do was look past the deformities, into Na'il's heart.

Then they would see a boy, rejected by the world, but made beautiful by God.

The Highly Sensitive Person – HSP

This trait is not a new discovery, but an often misunderstood one.

Being HSP means that your nervous system is more sensitive to subtleties. Sight, hearing and sense of smell are usually keener. The brain processes the information and reflects on it longer and more intense.

This trait is often mislabeled as shyness, introversion, inhibitedness or fearfulness.
In cultures where being tough and outgoing is seen as 'ideal', HSP is not seen as a positive trait, especially not in men.

Because HSP processes incoming information from the five senses differently and more carefully, noise and crowds quickly become overwhelming. The result is overstimulation and becoming stressed out.

The HSP tendency to reflect on things makes them intuitive, creative, conscientious and concerned about others.
They pick out subtle cues in others through looks, tones, gestures and innuendos.

You can read more about the Highly Sensitive Person on a very good website from Elaine Aron: http://www.hsperson.com

Good books for further reading

◊ Westberg, Granger E.. *Good Grief*. Gift ed. Minneapolis: Augsburg Fortress Publishers, 2004.

◊ Dunn, Bill, and Kathy Leonard. *Through a Season of Grief: Devotions for Your Journey from Mourning to Joy*. Waco, TX: Thomas Nelson, 2004.

◊ Chalfant, Nancy Doyle. *Child of Grace: A Mother's Life Changed by a Daughter's Special Needs*. Columbia: H. Shaw, 1988.

◊ Harris, Trudy. *Glimpses of Heaven: True Stories of Hope and Peace at the End of Lifes Journey*. Grand Rapids, MI: Revell, 2008.

◊ Johnson, Barbara. *Splashes of Joy in the Cesspools of Life*. Lrg ed. Waco, TX: Thomas Nelson, 1996.

◊ Johnson, Barbara. *Fresh Elastic for Stretched-out Mums*. Grand Rapids, Michigan: Zondervan, 1996.

◊ Lush, Jean , and Pam Vredevelt. *Women and Stress*. Eleventh printing ed. Grand Rapids, Michigan: Revell, 2002.

◊ Newenhuyse, Elizabeth Cody. *Sometimes I Feel Like Running Away from Home*. Minneapolis: Bethany House Publishers, 1993.

◊ Swindoll, Charles R.. *Stress Fractures*. Harpenden: Scripture Press, 1991.

◊ Swindoll, Charles R.. *Encourage Me*. Grand Rapids, Michigan: Zondervan, 1993.

◊ Swindoll, Charles R.. *Three Steps Forward, Two Steps Back*. Revised ed. Waco, TX: Thomas Nelson, 1998.

◊ Swindoll, Charles R.. *God's Provision In Time Of Need*. Waco, TX: Thomas Nelson, 2001.

◊ Williams, Sarah. *The Shaming Of The Strong: The Challenge of an Unborn Life*. Colorado Springs, CO: Kingsway Communications Ltd., 2006.

MLA formatting by BibMe.org.

Rain or shine, Na'il always wanted to be outside!

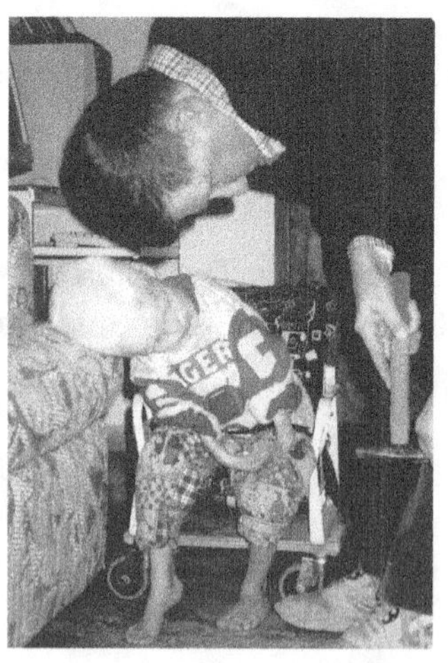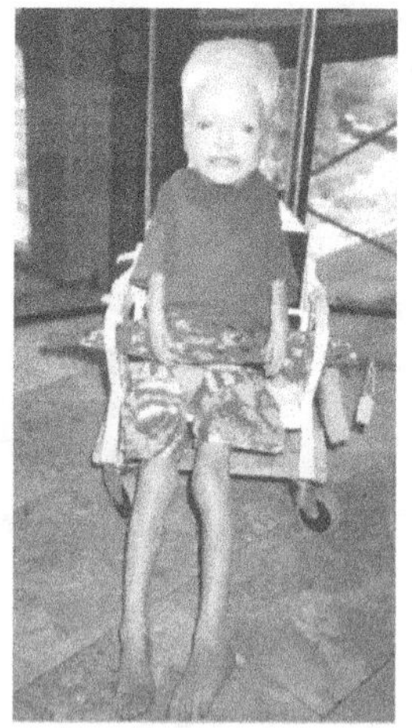

One Shabbat morning, Na'il found a
ballpoint. As he had learned in school, he
held it in his mouth, and he first tested it on
his legs. (In this picture he sits in a doll
buggy.) Then he moved to the wall. Now
that was really fun!

A child with such a mischievous look on his
face - you can't but give him a big hug!

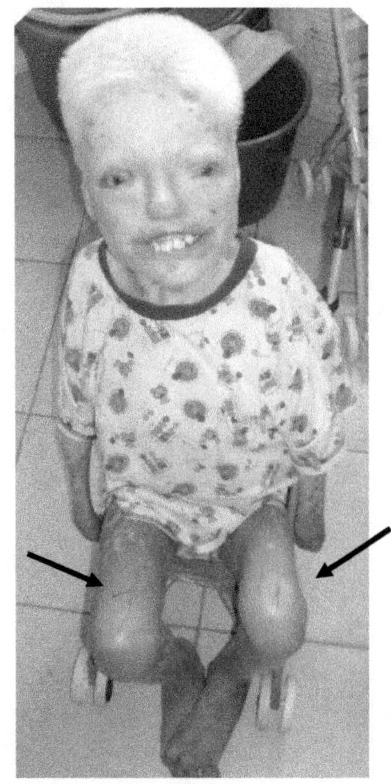

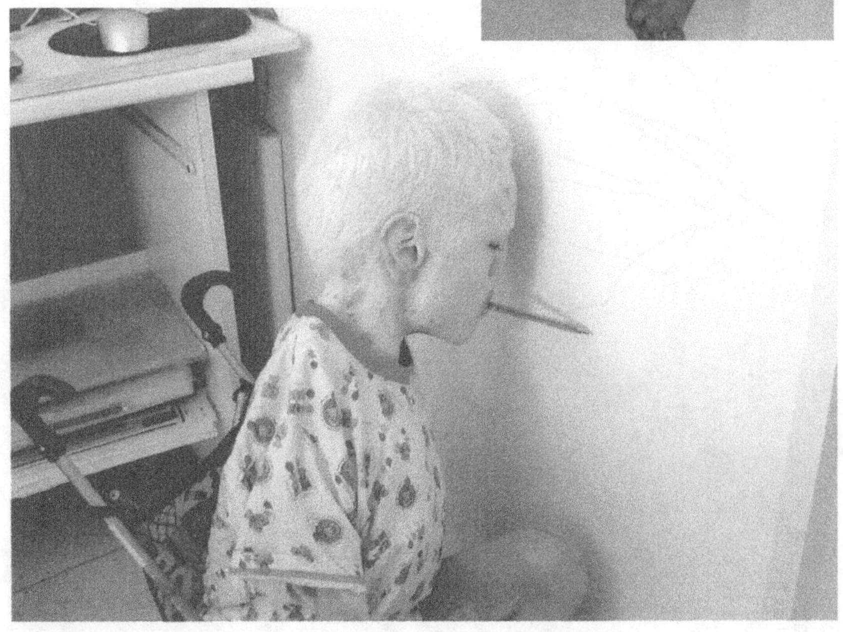